Venice

344 ILLUSTRATIONS

> *I gaze on Venice*
> *with joy, on that great*
> *Being born from the womb*
> *of the sea, like Pallas from*
> *the head of Jove*

"Journey to Italy" W. Gœthe, Rome 11.09.1786

St. Mark's Basilica.

STORTI EDIZIONI

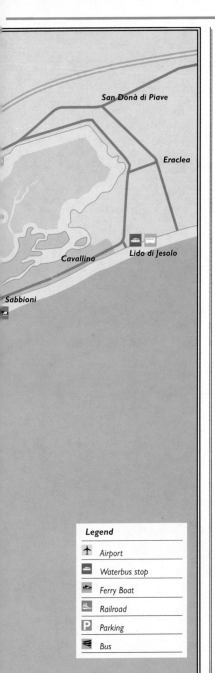

TRANSIT CONNECTIONS

Jesolo - Venice:
Bus, 1h.

Punta Sabbioni - Venice:
Motorship, 35'.

Airport "Marco Polo" - Venice (P.le Roma):
Bus, 35'.

Mestre - Venice:
Train, Bus, 10'.

S.Giuliano - Venice (F.ta Nuove):
Waterbus, 35'.

Fusina - Venice:
Motorship, 35'.

Chioggia - Venice:
Motorship, 1h., Bus, 1h,15'.

Padua - Venice:
Bus, Train, 1h.

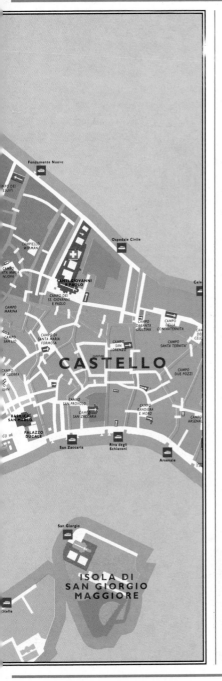

ITINERARIES

1 ST. MARK'S SQUARE
ST. MARK'S CHURCH
DOGE'S PALACE

2 ST. MARK'S BASIN
ST. GEORGE
GRAND CANAL

3 ACCADEMIA GALLERIES
CHURCH OF LA SALUTE

4 SAN ZACCARIA
COLLEONI MONUMENT
ARSENAL

5 RIALTO
CA' PESARO
CA' D'ORO

6 CA' REZZONICO
SAN ROCCO
I FRARI

7 MURANO
BURANO
TORCELLO
LIDO
CHIOGGIA

DISTRICTS

SAN MARCO
CASTELLO
CANNAREGIO
SAN POLO
SANTA CROCE
DORSODURO
GIUDECCA

HISTORICAL INTRODUCTION

In the course of a long historical process begun when the Roman Empire first showed signs of decadence, the Tenth Region (X Regio), that is, Venetia et Histria, became one of the most tormented areas of the Empire. Life in this region became ever more dangerous: the population learned to flee to the islands of the Lagoon. The great invasion of the Lombards in 568, during which both Aquileia and Altinium equally fell victim, was only the last violent stage of that long historical process. Perhaps it is from this moment that we may date the birth of Venice - not just as a city, but as a type of lagoon-civilisation: the refugees, in fact, were never to return to the mainland they had abandoned. In the year 584 when the Eastern Empire, undertaking the reconquest of a part of the Italian territories, created the Exarchate of Ravenna, the community of the Lagoon passed under the direct sovereignty of Byzantium. Successive events, however, were to reduce this sovereignty to a formality. With the election of Doge Agnello Partecipazio, the Byzantine party prevailed; this faction declared itself dependent on Byzantium although it knew quite well that the distance which separated Venice from the centre of the Eastern

Fishing hut

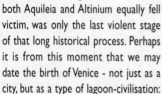

Marciana Library, Venice. The first residential settlements at Rialto. 16th-century paper codices

Venice's lagoon seen from the air

Empire would reduce this dependence to hollow formality, and would do little more than protect the community de jure from the expansionist policy of the Franks. This difficult policy of equilibrium translated itself into a state of strong social tension, in which changes in power usually came about in a violent form. Meanwhile the Venetians, who initially had been modest producers and suppliers of salt to the mainland immediately adjacent to the Lagoon, now became large-scale dealers and later enthusiastic merchants, who set about seeking ever longer and more hazardous trade routes.

Nonetheless, it was necessary to liberate the Upper Adriatic from the continuous threats of the Narentani, the Slav pirates, as well as the Middle and Lower Adriatic from the disturbing activities and irksome competition of the Saracens.

CONSTRUCTIONAL DIAGRAM:

1. *Bulkhead pilings that served as external barriers designed to keep out the canal water.*
2. *6000 piles that supported the Zatterone.*
3. *The platform itself.*
4. *Masonry.*
5. *Average water level.*
6. *Bottom of the canal.*

Rialto Bridge foundations

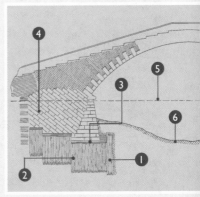

Nearly two centuries thus passed before the Dogeship finally succeeded in gathering sufficiently strong forces to inflict a mortal and decisive blow on the Slav pirates. In 991, Doge Pietro Orseolo II, seeing his opportunity in the rebellion of peoples of Venetian extraction resident on the other shore who did not wish to be subject to the Croatian king, intervened with a large army, disembarked at Zara and liberated all the immediate inland territory. He then pushed on southward against the Narentani, forcing them into signing a peace treaty near Split.

Following a political strategy which was destined to be imitated by their successors, the Venetians, far from proceeding to a true territorial conquest, limited themselves to possession of easily-maintained key points on the coast, granting the populace an ample measure of autonomy.

Between 1140 and 1160 the office of Doge definitely lost its monarchial character, and all political and administrative powers passed into the hands of the Maggior Consiglio (Great Council), composed of forty-five members, an institution which had developed from a smaller body called the Consiglio dei Sapienti (Council of the Wise). A Minor Consiglio (Lesser Council), of six members only, exercised the executive power.

It was during this period that the city assumed its unique physiognomy, with its political, religious and social

Pushkyn Museum, Moscow. Antonio Canaletto (1697-1768), the Feast of the Sensa

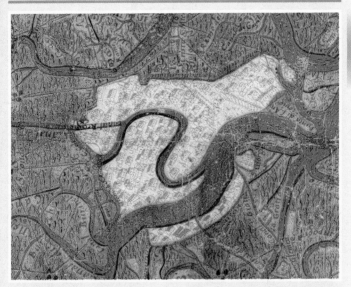

Ancient map of Venice

centre at San Marco, and its commercial centre at Rialto, linked to one another by the Mercerie, the city's main artery.

The struggle against the Normans, taken up by Doge Domenico Selvo (1071-1084 and by his successor Vitale Falier (1084-1096), assured free commerce with the Apulian ports where the Venetians renewed their grain supplies, and guaranteed free navigation to even more distant places. In addition, it indirectly favoured the Byzantine Empire as well.

Thus, as a mark of recognition of Venice's help and collaboration, Emperor Alexius I Comnenus conceded special privileges to Venetian commercial activity in Byzantium and other important localities. Things were complicated, however, by the presence in these markets of Genoa and Pisa.

Wall section near the entrance to Doge's Palace. Two details

Doge's Palace, Great Council. J. Palma the Y., Crusaders Assault Constantinople

In 1171, Emperor Manuel Comnenus I, relying on the support of Genoa and Pisa, tried to expel the Venetians from the Empire, arresting those Venetian citizens found there and confiscating all their goods. The Venetians did not respond until later: on the occasion of the Fourth Crusade (1202-04), for which they supplied arms.

The crusaders arrived in the East and instead of liberating the Holy Land, they sacked and conquered Byzantium itself, a flagrant act of piracy, though not considered such by contemporaries nor by the noble members of the expedition, who actually proposed that Doge Enrico Dandolo should assume the Imperial Purple. However he did not permit himself to be so easily flattered, but rather contented himself with retaining possession of certain commercial bases, and of numerous islands of the Aegean Sea, Mothoni and Corone as well as Crete.

Attempts continued by the richest and most powerful families of the city to seize power in order to hand it on to their sons, but newly-framed laws were destined to hinder such deviations.

As time passed various political plots failed, such as Marin Bocconio's in 1299, Bajamonte Tiepolo's and the Querini brothers' in 1310; and later, the most famous of all, Marin Falier's in 1354. In the meantime, in 1310, the Consiglio dei Dieci (Council of Ten) had been

The Return of the Doge (det.).

created specifically in order to control the power of the patricians. Created as a temporary body as a result of this long series of plots, it eventually became a permanent fixture; and before very long it had become the most powerful institution of the

Republic and investigated all matters which could might prove harmful to the State, with a secret police of its own. As depicted in chronicles of the time, the latter left little or nothing further to be desired by modern secret police systems.

Venice and Genoa were in conflict in the mid 13th century; commercial conflict between them was gradually transformed into an armed struggle. This conflict culminated in the violent battle of St. Jean d'Acre, in which Genoa's fleet was defeated by that of Venice, led by

Doge's Palace, Great Council. P. Veronese. The Victorious Return of Doge A. Contarini after Victory of Chioggia.

Lorenzo Tiepolo and Andrea Zeno. There was a brief period of peace, but the struggle become more violent than ever in the 14th century. The final episodes of the struggle with Genoa developed in the Upper Adriatic, threatening Venice itself. After the defeats at Pola and Chioggia, the Republic was still capable of finding sufficient resources and of concentrating on a last and mighty effort, the result of which was the definitive and total defeat of the Genoese - at Chioggia, once more - by Venetian forces captained by Vettor Pisani. The Peace of Turin, signed during the following year, 1381, signalled the beginning of Genoa's subsequent ruin.

Once this dangerous rival had been eliminated, a new threat began to cast its shadow over the famous Venetian trade routes: the Turks began to press upon the whole of Asia Minor, encircling the exhausted Eastern Empire. Thus they proceeded into the Mediterranean, hindering free trade with their acts of piracy. The Venetians, knowing full well that their forces were unequal to such an adversary, once more showed themselves wise in the intuition that their best policy consisted of a state of armed neutrality. They then sought compensation on the mainland, where trade relations with the cities of the Po river basin and Northern Europe acquired the same importance for them as commerce overseas.

Some historians are accustomed to juxtapose dates, noting, for example, that the taking of Brescia in 1426 was contemporaneous with the loss of Thessalonica; expansion towards the Adda (1432-1453) took place at exactly the time when the Turks, led by Mahomet II, inflicted the mortal blow on the Eastern Empire (1453-1454); not to mention the war with Ferrara (1481), contemporaneous with conquest of the Polesine, which (except for Ferrara) was assigned to Venice at the Peace of Bagnolo in 1484. These events led to an anti-Venetian coalition which saw the forces of half of Europe united against her.

Inevitably, as trade in the Orient diminished, mainland trade had to increase correspondingly. This required investment of private capital which resulted in the progressive deterioration of public finances.

Doge's Palace, Great Council:
the "Conquest of Padua" by J. Palma the Y.

Doge's Palace, the Great Council, the Defense of Brescia by J.Tintoretto

Neither in Italy nor abroad could the birth of a powerful State in northern or central Italy be tolerated. The only entities which could aspire to such a role were the Dukedom of Milan, the Republic of Venice and, in a certain sense, the States of the Church. Every state at one time or another had its great man and its moment, and every state sooner or later failed in the attempt, thanks to the united forces of the others. What was impossible to achieve in 1500 came about three hundred years later.

Against its own wishes, the Republic had already assumed a territorial and political dimension disproportionate to is own inherent powers. The forming of the League of Cambrai was

therefore fatal. All of the member groups had their good reasons to wish for the end of the Republic, and the serious defeat at Agnadello in 1509, one of the most tragic in Venetian history, in many ways seems to have been final. Only internal discord among the victors succeeded in saving Venice from ruin. But by this time the city had already reached a point where it was forced to play a secondary role in European politics.

The downward swing of the arc of Venetian fortunes starts here. In the years spanning the end of the 15th and the beginning of the 16th century, the discovery of America opened up a new chapter in European history. The economic centre of gravity shifted from the internal seas of Europe (the North Sea, the Baltic, the Mediterranean), to the ocean: Lisbon, Seville, Rotterdam, London, took the place of cities which up to then had been of first rank - namely, Lubeck, Genoa, Venice.

This event is incorrectly held to be the starting point of the decline of Venetian commerce. At any rate, more than a hundred years were to pass before the new Atlantic sea-routes became commercially competitive. Venice continued to import from the Orient and to export to Occidental markets, but with ever-increasing difficulties. The discovery of America was less damaging than Turkish pressure which, from a military threat, became a commercial one. Private merchants preferred to invest their capital in other, more secure projects. From time to time the Republic would look for allies against the Turks, but always and inevitably, it had to bear the brunt of the fighting. The account of events linked to the defeat at Preveza in 1538 is noteworthy; equally so, the one telling of the victory at Lepanto in 1571, glorified and immortalised by the canvases of famous painters. However, both were marginal episodes in a losing battle. In reality, like all historical processes, economic decline was slow though inexorable, and at times even seemed to cease. The politics of renunciation was destined to be repudiated by brilliant (though ultimately unproductive) events in the city's history. Thanks

Doge's Palace, College. The Battle of Lepanto by P. Veronese

alone to mediation by Henry IV, king of France, war with Pope Paul V was avoided (1605-1607). The Pope had issued an Interdict against Venice as a protest against the arrest of two priests guilty of common crimes in Venice. The origin of this great tension lay in the recent occupation of Ferrara, the perennial bone of contention between Venice and the Papacy, by Clement VIII, on the death of the last Duke of Ferrara, Alfonso d'Este, in 1597.

Correr Museum, Venice. J. Grevembroch, Two Ladies (detail.)

The defense of the island of Crete against the Turks would be one of the last episodes in which the Republic once again showed a decisive will to stand against the preordained course of events. The siege of Candia was protracted for a quarter of a century, from 1645 to 1669, but in the end even this valuable source of financial advantages for the Venetian economy would be lost. Dalmatia still remained, and thanks to the brilliant campaigns of Francesco Morosini, the Morea was liberated and passed into Venetian hands with the Treaty of Karlowitz in 1699. For this feat, Morosini would receive the title of the Peloponnesiaco.

Correr Museum, Venice. V. M. Coronelli, Standard Bearers in the Doge's Cortège (detail.)

Even this was only a short-lived conquest for with the Treaty of Passarowitz in 1712, the Morea was restored once more to the Turks. From then onwards Venice's military and political neutrality was to become all-pervading.

The city lived on memories; music conservatories flourished, gambling houses multiplied, every possible occasion was an excuse for a celebration; visits from illustrious foreign personages furnished occasions for bull-fights and other entertainment.

Toward the last years of the century world history becomes so rich with events that the end of the Republic passes almost unnoticed: on 12th March 1797 the last Doge, Lodovico Manin, was deposed. The Municipal democracy which substituted the government of the Republic lasted on into October of the same year, when the Peace Treaty of Campoformio was signed, by which Napoleon gave up Venice to Austria in exchange for the left bank of the Rhine and Milan.

ARTISTIC INTRODUCTION

The development of the city of Venice is closely linked to its political and commercial relations with the Near East and with Constantinople, in particular. Nearby Ravenna is another point of reference.

Byzantine art spreads through Italy in contact with the declining Roman world, suggesting new expressive motifs. After the first period of its establishment was over and a certain security and independence achieved, Venice substituted its humble houses of brick, wood and mud, its constructions of a defensive nature and its turreted castles, with a new and more splendid kind of building, the model for which was clearly copied from Byzantine architecture. Columns, capitals, rare marbles, fabrics and spices all found a place in the hold of their ships. Eastern and Ravenna craftsmen were called to Venice, both by the state itself and by private citizens, to supervise the work, and it must have been these who initiated the untrained local craftsmen into the secrets and the skills of building and decoration. In those early centuries the city thus took on a Byzantine aspect.

Little now remains of this kind of building in the city. The location of surviving examples in particular parts of the city indicates the area where it first

Accademia Galleries, Procession of the Cross in St. Mark's Square, Gentile Bellini

began to develop: from San Marco to Rialto by internal ways, and along the Grand Canal from San Polo to San Zan Degolà. This is the period of the great doges - the Orseolos, Domenico Contarini and Sebastiano Ziani.

Thus we come to around the middle of the 13th century. From this point onwards the city gradually took shape both architecturally and decoratively according to the taste and culture which was common to Italy as a whole.

GOTHIC PERIOD:
from the second half of the 13th century to the second half of the 15th century (circa 1470); from the period of transition to flamboyant.

St. Mark's Basilica. Pala d'Oro, detail

EARLY RENAISSANCE:
from the second half of the 15th century (circa 1460-1470) to the beginning of the 16th century (1525-1530).

RENAISSANCE:
for the whole of the sixteenth century. About 1580 new motifs emerged which foreshadowed the evolution of taste toward the

BAROQUE:
17th century. The evolution of Baroque brought increasingly richer forms of decoration.

ROCOCÒ:
the Settecento (18th century).

NEO-CLASSICAL:
the beginning of the 19th century.

ITINERARY

SAN MARCO

St. Mark's Basilica. St Alipius
Portal. Main façade (1265).

Clock Tower.
A statue of the Moors.

Rio Dei Fabbri

C. S. Zulian

C. Morosina

Rio

Scoacamini

Rio Ferali

Campo
S. Zulian

Rio Dei
Scoacamini

C. Preti

Delle Colonne

Calle Fiubera

Mercerial De

Procuratie

Rio T.
C. s.
Gallo

Calle Fabbri

C. Cavalletto

Delle

Rio

Ft. Orseolo

Bacino
Orseolo

Rio

C.B. Cappello Ne

C. Selvadego

Procuratie Vecchie

Bocca di
Piazza

Piazza San

S. Moisè

C. Ascensione

Procuratie Nuov

Rio

Palazzo Reale
della

Zec

Giardinetti Reali

San Marco
Vallaresso

San Ma
Giardin

Clock Tower.
Lion of St Mark.

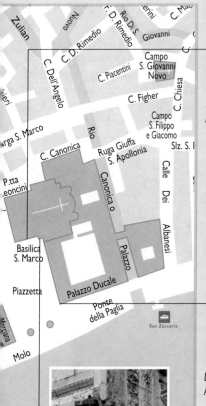

South façade of the Basilica.
Acritan Pilasters.

Doge's Palace, southwest corner.
Adam and Eve.

St Mark's Basilica, south façade.
The Tetrarchs.

The present shape of **Piazza San Marco,** the city's political, religious and social centre, was gradually created over the course of ten centuries in the history of the Venetian Republic. In spite of the many and inevitable transformations of buildings, the square on the whole has maintained a unified character, although it is composed of two spacious intercommunicating areas: the actual Piazza itself and the Piazzetta. The first layout of the square goes back to the beginning of the dukedom, that is the beginning of the 9th century. In 832 the first church dedicated to the Evangelist St. Mark, was consecrated. According to legend, the remains of the saint were stolen by two Venetian seamen from a monastery in Alexandria in Egypt, and brought to Venice. The symbol of the winged lion, proper attribute of the Evangelist, became the symbol of the city. St. Mark became its patron saint.

The church was called the church of the Partecipazio family because it had been built at the wish of Agnello Partecipazio, whose family gave as many as

St. Mark's Square, aerial view

St. Mark's Basilica, façade.

seven doges to the city between 811 and 939; it was destroyed in 976 when the people, in revolt, set fire to the ducal castle in an effort to force Doge Pietro IV Candiano out of it. His successor, Pietro Orseolo, began reconstruction and restoration of the buildings that had been destroyed. At the same time buildings of more modest proportions were being raised round the square, which was still bounded by Rio Batario, and was still unpaved. The campanile stood detached like a tower

The Loggetta by Jacopo Sansovino. A sculpture

Basilica seen from the Loggetta

of defense, a watch-tower, on the spot where it still stands today. Only a few fragmentary traces of this period remain, not sufficient to reconstruct even sketchily the aspect of the square in these centuries except by referring to the buildings on the island of Torcello. Near the Porta della Carta there are the remains of foundations and walls of a thickness not found in any other walls in the Ducal Palace, which would suggest that they belong to the original castle; in the Basilica itself there are capitals, stone screens, paterae, panels and balustrades, cornices and various fragments that date from the earlier buildings. More important evidence is to be seen in the sixteen little arcades at the base of the presbytery. They form the upper part of the underlying crypt; the workmanship of the four central columns seems to be earlier than that of the others. In 1063, during the reign of Domenico Contarini, work on the third and last of the Basilicas of St. Mark was begun. In 1071, on the death of the doge, the building was complete in all its essential structural elements, and in 1094 it was consecrated. This is the church which still exists today, successively enriched by decorations and facing in marble and mosaic. As such its exterior was columns and capitals within the embrasures of the five great doorways, and the bas-reliefs on the arches of the main doorway. And now each of the low hemispherical domes had been covered with a second dome of lead independent of the inner one, and crowned with lanterns in Eastern taste, accomplished throughout the preceding centuries.

With the increasing power of Venice

Meeting between Pope Alexander III, Doge Sebastiano Ziani and Emperor Frederick Barbarossa

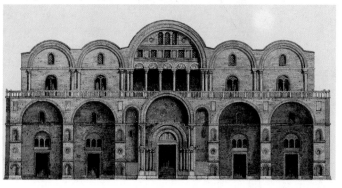

Saint Mark's Basilica. Possible original plan for the main façade

remarkably modified as compared with its original aspect.

In those days it must have appeared, even if imposing, bare and severe in its austere brickwork. The work of completion ceased definitely in the fifteenth century with the splendid crowning of foliage and the pinnacles and little niches on the upper arches of the façades. These were the finishing touches following the placing of the double row of the square gradually took on an aspect of greater splendour. Doge Sebastiano Ziani (1172-1178) commissioned a new layout for it, and by filling in Rio Batario doubled the space in front of the Basilica. The two Columns, which belong to this period, mark the limit of the space occupied by the Piazzetta towards the Basin. They consist of two monoliths which were brought from the East and placed on octagonal stepped bases, decorated with carvings showing the various crafts. Their great capitals respectively support a winged lion and the statue of St Theodore with the dragon.

Chronicles of the time tell us that the work of setting up these columns was entrusted to a certain Nicolò Barattieri, who underwrote the immense cost of the work in exchange for permission from the Republic to keep between the two columns, a public gaming table. Gambling has been much in vogue in Venice in every period, though it has often been forbidden. The buildings around the Square gradually lost their

defensive character (especially the Doge's Palace), a sure sign of complete safety from attack, whether from within or from outside. It is certain that Doge Ziani's palace was enlarged on the lagoon side, where the highest powers of the Venetian government, the Great Council, met in the Sala del Piovego. Only at the end of the 13th century was there a need to thoroughly rebuild the Palace. The work was begun around the middle of the 14th century, when the wing facing the waterfront was rebuilt to encompass the whole of the old palace. On the ground floor portico

Piazzetta with its two columns

Venice's coat-of-arms

there runs a loggia upon which rests the enormous volume of the Great Council Hall. On the side facing the Piazzetta the width of the façade reached as far as the sixth arch.

During the reign of Francesco Foscari, from 1424, the building of the section extending from the sixth arch to the Porta della Carta was begun.

Doge's Palace. 14th-century capital (detail)

The city as seen in an 18th-century engraving

The Clock Tower

Between 1496 and 1499 the **Clock Tower** was built, apparently according to a design by Mauro Coducci.

The street of the Mercerie, which comes up from Rialto, opens into the Square by passing through the tower archway. This street, which originated in the first layout of the city, united the political and commercial centres.

Between 1500 and 1506, Pietro Lombardo added the two wings, while the upper floors were built much later, in 1755, by Giorgio Massari. Besides telling the time, the great gilt, blue enamel clock face also shows the movement of the sun and phases of the moon with the signs of the zodiac. The actual mechanism was made by Paolo and Carlo Ranieri, called expressly from Reggio.

On the upper terrace there is a

Moors and city coat-of-arms

bell and two statues in bronze called the "Moors". By means of a mechanism connected with the clock, they swing round and strike the bell.

The work of rebuilding still went on in the Square. One after another all the old houses of the Procurators were pulled down, and between 1496 and 1530 Mauro Coducci, Bartolomeo Bon, and Guglielmo dei Grigi built the **Procuratie Vecchie** from

Clock Tower. Clock

the end of the Mercerie to the corner at the opposite end of the Square and up to the church of San Geminiano. At first it only had one floor (the second was added later on); it now presents an unbroken row of fifty arches on the ground level and double the number of windows on the upper floors. The motif which inspired the façade of this palace quite certainly derived from the previous Byzantine construction, several times rebuilt in later centuries, containing **the Zecca**, or Mint; this was transferred from Rialto to San Marco in

Clock Tower. Zodiac

1277. From 1537 to 1545 a new building designed by Jacopo Sansovino was erected. Here the most celebrated Venetian money, the gold ducat, or sequin, was coined; this coin was honoured in all European and Eastern markets. Today the building is used as a depository and reading room for the adjacent Marciana Library.

The **Marciana Library**, too, was built by Jacopo Sansovino, who began it in 1537 with the part nearest the

Campanile. The building limits the west side of the Piazzetta. The work, which went on until 1545, was interrupted when part of the vault fell in. Sansovino was put in prison but two years later, freed and reappointed, he carried on the work until 1554, when he succeeded in completing it as far as the sixteenth arch.

In 1583 Vincenzo Scamozzi took on the work and completed it, turning the corner towards the Basin and joining it up with the Mint. Sansovino detached the edifice from the Campanile and established a new line, further back from the one formed by the Orseolo Hospice, for the buildings which later would reach the other end of the Square. Sansovino's design was taken up by Scamozzi who, having pulled down the Orseolo Hospice, began work on the Procuratie Nuove.

View of the Grand Canal from the wharf. Night

Jacopo Sansovino. Library

The **Procuratie Nuove** were begun in 1586, carrying on the traditional scheme with the arcade on ground level. On the architect's death in 1616 it had reached the tenth arch and in 1634 was continued by Baldassare Longhena, who finally completed it. Since the 13th century there has been a Loggia in the Piazzetta dei Leoncini, called the Ridotto dei Nobili, which was transferred later on to the foot of the Campanile. Between 1537 and 1549 this little building was remade by Jacopo Sansovino. Later on, in 1663, the side arches were turned into doorways and on the front a terrace was added, with a balustrade reached by a flight of steps in the centre. The building was completely destroyed when the Campanile collapsed in 1902; it was rebuilt with the material recovered, in accordance with the original design.

St Mark's. Campanile.

The old pavement of Saint Mark's Square, in red brick herringbone, remained unchanged from 1264 to the early 18th century when, in accordance with the taste of the period it was thought necessary to give a more splendid appearance to the Square, and the bricks were exchanged for slabs of grey trachite from the Euganean Hills, with wide strips of white marble inlaid to compose a severe and plain pattern. Andrea Tirali supervised the work between 1723 and 1735.

The **Campanile of Saint Mark** had been restored more than once, and also partly rebuilt at various times: the belfry and the spire, in particular. In 1902 it collapsed, but rebuilding was begun at once according to the old design, and it was completed in 1912. Of the five bells the most celebrated is the one known as the "Marangona", whose name comes from the fact that it rang for the beginning and the end of the day's work for the "Marangoni", carpenters (and for craftsmen of all the guilds and corporations in general).

St. Mark's Square, looking west.

St. Mark's Basilica.
The Gothic crowning (detail)

St. Mark's Square, looking east.

St. Mark's Basilica and the Horses

Basilica of St Mark. The plan is a Greek cross. The atrium or narthex goes round three sides of its lower part. The piers of the nave support five huge domes. The façade is planned in two orders, the lower one consisting of five great deeply-set doorways leading into the narthex, while the upper one consists of the

same number of arch-
es. Between the two
orders there is a
terrace with copies of
the four bronze horses in

the centre; these were brought from Byzantium after the fall of the city during the Fourth Crusade. In the lower order from left to right: Arch of Saint Alipius, added to the building in the 13th century. In the lunette of the first doorway there is the only extant mosaic from the original decorations of the façade; it

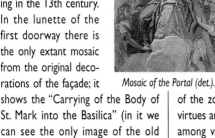

Mosaic of the Portal (det.).

shows the "Carrying of the Body of St. Mark into the Basilica" (in it we can see the only image of the old basilica in existence). In the intrados and extrados of the arches there is an important series of carvings which pass from shapes and subjects inspired by the Romanesque carving of the early 13th century to the unmistakably Gothic floral forms and figures of the first half of the 14th century. Following in order from the smallest to the largest arch: confronted or fighting animals within floral motifs; hunting and battle scenes; the months and the signs of the zodiac; figures symbolising the virtues and beatitudes; Venetian crafts; among volutes and pierced paterae, Prophets and Christ blessing. Set on the corner close to the Porta della Carta is the Group of the Tetrarchs, called the "Moors" - four figures of

St. Mark's Basilica. Portal (detail). Above: detail of the mosaic

St. Mark's Basilica, south side. The Tetrarchs

warriors in porphyry; they are, it seems, the four emperors who were allies of Diocletian. In front, standing detached, there are the two Pilasters from Acre, war booty brought by the Venetians after the conquest of Saint-Jean d'Acre in Syria, in 1257. Recent archaeological discoveries, though, have determined their origin in Byzantium. On the side facing the Piazzetta dei Leoncini, there is the Porta dei Fiori, in which the thir-teenth-century architecture is grafted onto the older building. We go into the interior of the Basilica; the front part and the left wing are rhythmically spaced by pointed arches alternating

St. Mark's Basilica narthex.
The Evangelists: Matthew and Mark,
Luke and John

with small blind domes, while the right wing is completely closed in, being taken up by the Zen Chapel and the Baptistery.

The mosaic decoration of the vaults belongs to the original building and was carried out beginning as far back as the 13th century. Starting from the right the mosaics illustrate: "The Creation of the World", in twenty-four scenes, *"The Story of Cain and Abel"*, *"Stories of Noah and the Flood"*, *"The Building of the Tower of Babel"*, *"The Story of Abraham"*, *"The Story of Joseph"*, *"The Story of Moses"*. We pass through the great central apse-shaped doorway and go into the church. The great nave and transept are all contained in the space created by the huge isolated piers. The two aisles lie along the sides, separated from the main body of the church by the women's galleries.

The apse area consists of the great central apse with the high altar and the two side chapels of St. Peter

Floor mosaic

Narthex, Domes: Creation, Abraham, Joseph

and St. Clement, flanked by the two en-trances to the crypt. Going around the church south wards from the right we find the **Baptistery**, also known as the Church of the Putti, which communicates with the Zen Chapel. This part of the Basilica underwent certain changes in the 14th century, according to designs by Jacopo Sansovino.

On the wall facing the entrance is the monument to the doge Andrea Dandolo. On the walls and in the domes numerous mosaics of the mid 14th century show *"The Life of St. John the Baptist and the Childhood of Jesus"*. After the Baptistery we come to the **Treasury of Saint Mark's**, displayed in three inter-communicating rooms: the Sanctuary, the Ante-Treasury and the Treasury. In these three rooms we find one of the richest and most important collections of Byzantine and Oriental goldsmiths' craft, being

St. Mark's Basilica. The Baptistery

St. Mark's Basilica. The Presbytery with the the Pala d'Oro

mainly of the period subsequent to the conquest of Constantinople and Tyre by the Venetians.

The Presbytery is divided from the nave by the Gothic Iconostasis, above the architrave of which are the statues of the Virgin, of St. John the Evangelist, and of the Twelve Apostles, sculpted by Dalle Masegne (1394). On the high altar is **the Pala d'Oro** (golden altar screen), rectangular in form and measuring 3.5 m. by 2.4 m, a work in precious metal of inestimable value in which the figures of saints and virgins animate the decorative rhythm, which is further enriched by enamels, gems and gold-mounted objects. The whole is the fruit of long years of work in precious metals, and assumed its present aspect in the 14th century.

Immediately afterwards comes the Chapel of St. Isidore, constructed on a rectangular plan with a barrel vault. On the end wall we find the sarcophagus containing the relics of the Saint, surmounted by the richly decorated archisolium. The fourteenth-century mosaics show episodes in the life of St. Isidore and *"The Translation of the Body of the Saint from Chios to Venice"* by Doge Domenico Michiel 1125).

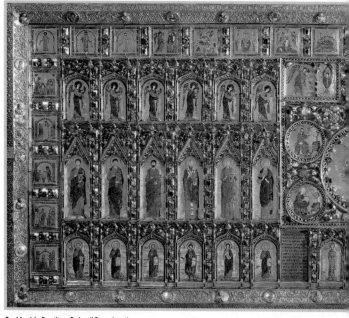

St. Mark's Basilica. Pala d'Oro, detail
Below: Pala d'Oro, detail

To one side opens the Chapel of the Madonna of the Mascoli, which belonged to a Venetian confraternity consisting of men only. The cycle of mosaics showing the Life of the Virgin, started in about 1430 by Michele Giambono and finished, it would seem, after designs by Jacopo Bellini, Andrea Mantegna and Andrea del Castagno, is particularly important.

The **mosaic work** of the Basilica, started under the dogeship of Domenico Selvo (1071-1084), of which some fragments remain, was continued and developed in the 12th and 13th centuries, while cer-tain parts were renovated later. The mosaics extend over an area of approximately 4,500 sq. m.

Starting at the entrance, the Arch of Paradise: *"Scenes from the Last Judgement"* (16th century). Above the door: *"The Saviour between the Virgin and St Mark"* (13th century). The Arch of the Apocalyse: *"Scenes from the life of St John the Evangelist"* (16th century). In the dome of the Pente-cost: *"Descent of the Holy Spirit upon the Apostles"* (12th century). In the two side aisles are shown scenes from the lives of the Apostles and their martyrdoms; in addition,

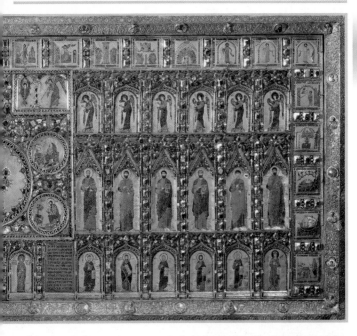

St. Mark's Basilica. Pala d'Oro: Entrance in Jerusalem

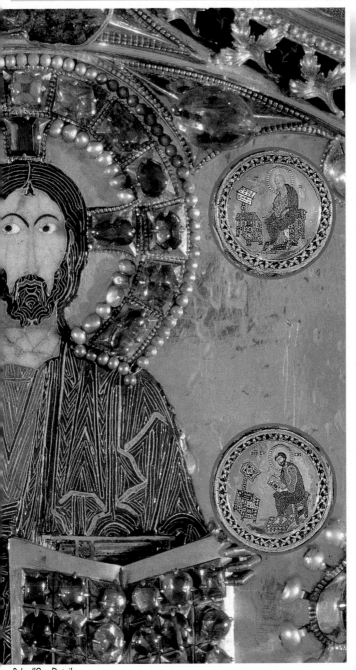

Pala d'Oro. Details

on the left wall there are five divisions in which are represented: *"Jesus blessing, between four Prophets"* (13th century), and on the right the same number of divisions with *"The Virgin praying, between four Prophets"* (13th century). While the mosaics of the left aisle were redone with the same subjects in the 16th and 17th centuries, those of the right aisle are of the 12th and 13th centuries. On the left wall at the end, *"Paradise with the Trinity"* (16th century); on the right *"Jesus praying in the garden"* (13th century).

On the central arch *"The Passion of Christ"* is represented in five scenes (middle of the 12th century). The great central Ascension dome is dominated by the image of *"Christ in Glory surrounded by angels, the Virgin and the Twelve Apostles"*, by figures symbolising the Virtues and the Beatitudes, and finally, the Evangelists and the four holy rivers. These mosaics date back to the first half of the 13th century. They are among the finest mosaic works in all of Venice.

One then proceeds to the transept arches. On the left, we find *"Episodes from the Life of Christ"*; in particular, several miracles and the *"Last Supper"* (redone in the 16th century according to cartoons by Jacopo Tintoretto and Paolo Veronese). The right-hand arch presents other episodes from the life of Christ, including the *"Temptations of Satan"* (end of 12th to

St. Mark's Basilica. The south transept

beginning of 13th century). On the left wing of the transept is the San Giovanni cupola, depicting various episodes from the life of Saint John the Evangelist; on the lower section, figures of the Church Fathers (end of 12th century). Several figures, however, were redone at the beginning of the 18th century. On the terminal transept arch, beside the dome, on the upper tier, we see *"Episodes from the*

St. Mark's Basilica. Floor mosaic

life of the Virgin and Jesus" (nearly all from the late 12th or early 13th century). The lower tier shows *"Episodes from the life of Susanna"* and *"Christ's Miracles"* (those above the altar of the Virgin were redone in the 17th century). On the back wall we find the *"Geneological Tree of the Virgin"* done according to designs by Salviati (1542-1551). On the right wing of the transept we find the San Leonar-

St. Mark's Basilica right-hand nave. Virgin praying

St. Mark's Basilica right-hand nave. David and Solomon

do cupola, with figures of saints, of the 13th century, In the arch beside the dome, above the door of the Treasure, we see mosaics depicting *"Episodes from the life of the Virgin"* (redone in the 17th century). In the lower tier we see *"Discovery of the Body of Saint Mark"* (13th century). On the vault over the altar of the Sacrament, we find mosaics of the late 12th century illustrating *"Parables and Miracles of Christ"*. Some of these works were renovated in the 15th and 17th century. On the Presbytery arch, again *"Episodes from the life of Christ"* made according to a cartoon by Jacopo Tintoretto; in the centre, *"Resurrection of Christ"*. The Presbytery dome has mosaics symbolically representing the Christian message preannounced by the Prophets. All are contemporary with or just posterior to works in the Pentecost cupola: i.e., between the late 12th and early 13th century). The apse basin shows *"Christ Blessing"*; in the lower tier we find *"Saints"*, whose figures survive the early mosaic decorations commissioned by Doge Domenico Selvo (1071). Other mosaics present *"Episodes from the life of Saints Mark, Peter and Clement"*, also in the Presbytery.

St. Mark's Basilica. J. and P. Dalle Masegne, Iconostasis

The **Library,** rich with valuable manuscripts and incunabula, was founded by the legacy of Cardinal Bessarion (1468). In time other valuable works were added to it. We come to the entrance-hall, where at one time, lectors of philosophy and letters gave public lessons. The ceiling, designed and built by Cristoforo Rosa between 1550 and 1560, has a central section enriched by Titian's painting representing "Wisdom". From here, we enter the Hall of the Library, a vast room measuring 26,40 m. by 10.65 m.; the vaulted ceiling is subdivided into twenty-one round compartments On the walls, with numerous other paintings, is the series of the Philosophers in false niches, by Jacopo Tintoretto. The rarest of the books and manuscripts from the bequest of Cardinal Bessarion are on exhibition in the cases. Here are celebrated editions published by Aldus Manutius (the most famous Venetian printer, editor and publisher of the time and perhaps the most celebrated in all Europe), and also the Grimani Breviary from the end of the 15th century, precious for its one hundred and ten full-page illuminations.

Grimani Breviary. Two miniatures

The **Correr Museum**. This museum is situated in the rooms of the Procuratie Nuove entered from the staircase in the Napoleonic Wing at the opposite end of the Square facing the Basilica. The museum has two sections, the first with collections relevant to the history and customs of Venice (paintings, prints, documents, costumes, model ships, coins, arms and armour, standards, seals and sculptures); the second, called the Quadreria or painting collection, housing works particularly worthy of note by Paolo, Lorenzo and Stefano Veneziano, Jacobello del Fiore, Michele Giambono, the Vivarinis, Vittore Carpaccio, Giovanni and Gentile Bellini, Antonello da Messina and Cosmè Tura. Adjacent to the aforementioned rooms are the Archaeological Museum and the Museum of the Risorgimento.

Correr Museum. A. Maccagnini, Portrait of a Lady

Correr Museum. V. Carpaccio,
Young man with a red cap

Correr Museum. B. Estense,
Portrait of a nobleman

Correr Museum. Unknown artist of the 18th c. The Doge visits the square

(Page 56/57) Doge's Palace

(Page 56) Porta della Carta

(Page 56) Corner sculpture near the Porta della Carta illustrating Solomon's Judgement

(Page 57) Southwest corner sculpture showing Adam and Eve

(Page 57) Southeast corner sculpture showing Noah inebriated

View of Doge's Palace from the Piazzetta

Doge's Palace. Detail

The main entrance to the **Doge's Palace** is the one called the Porta della Carta, built between 1438 and 1443 by Giovanni and Bartolomeo Bon, in flamboyant Gothic style. It was once painted in blue, red and gold. The figure of Doge Francesco Foscari is shown kneeling before the Winged Lion, but the one we can see today is a copy of the original, which was destroyed at the time of the fall of the Republic.

The Porta della Carta leads straight to the cross-vaulted Foscari Arcade, which stands against the outside wall of the Basilica of St. Mark. In front is the Renaissance **Staircase of the Giants**, designed and built by Antonio Rizzo, chief architect of the Palace; it was begun in 1483.

By placing the staircase in a straight line with the Foscari Arch, the architect has created both a physical and metaphysical progression from the Piazzetta to the Porta della Carta and, through the Foscari Arch and up the stairs, to the Loggia above. On the landing at the top, widened by two spaces at the sides, the official investiture of the doge took place before he was presented to the people.

The two states on the balustrade, Mars and Neptune, are late works by Jacopo Sansovino. On the left of the stairway is the little Senators' Courtyard with its façade by Antonio Scarpagnino and Giorgio Spavento, done at the beginning of the 16th century.

The **Foscari Arch**, which stands in front of the Staircase, was begun during the reign of Foscari, and continued during the time of Doge Cristoforo

Moro. The two statues of Adam and Eve, in the niches, are by Antonio Rizzo: the originals are inside the Palace in the rooms of the Quarantia Criminal. On the right is the Great Courtyard with its two bronze wellheads cast between 1554 and 1559 by Alfonso Alberghetti and Nicolò dei Conti.

The two façades in brick correspond to the Hall of the Great Council and the Hall of the Scrutiny; they are the oldest, dating from the 14th and 15th centuries, when the respective parts of the Place were built; the large windows were put in at a later date. The third façade is Renaissance in style and belongs to the wing facing the Rio

Doge's Palace. The courtyard façade in Renaissance style

Doge's Palace. The Giants' staircase

di Palazzo. It was built after the great fire of 1483; at the same time the walls and interior decorations of the rooms were renovated and restored. The work was planned and begun by Antonio Rizzo, then continued after 1498 by the Lombardos. In 1516 it was taken up by Antonio Abbondi, called lo Scarpagnino. At the same time the new façade overlooking the Rio di Palazzo was built. The work went on for several years, and some parts were completed by the beginning of the 17th century with the help of Monopola, who also built the arcades on the ground floor on the two oldest façades. He completed the small north façade of the clock, after having removed the ancient Foscara Staircase. The visitor will find a walk along the Loggias of great interest - both the inner one and the outer one, towards the Piazzetta and lagoon. From the former we can reach the rooms, by means of the highly elaborate **Golden Staircase**, which today has lost a great deal of its former splendour. It was begun during the reign of Andrea Gritti (1523-39) from a design by Jacopo Sansovino, and finished by Scarpagnino in 1559. A great many artists collaborated in the work: the marble groups of the entrance archway ("*Hercules Killing the Hydra*", "*Atlas Supporting the World*") are by Tiziano Aspetti; the stucco work on the vaulted ceiling is by Alessandro Vittoria; the frescoes on the panels are by Battista Franco.

Doge's Palace. Golden Staircase

Doge's Palace. Erizzo Room

The **Doge's Apartment** rooms are now practically bare, preserving only the carved wooden ceiling and fireplaces, by the Lombardos. In their respective order we find the Hall of the Scarlatti, anteroom of the Ducal Counsellors; the Hall of the Shield or Maps, with all its geographical maps on the walls done by Francesco Griselllini and Giustino Menescardi; the Grimani Hall, with two paintings by Gerolamo da Ponte from Bassano: "*Circumcision*" and "*Ascent to Calvary*"; Erizzo Hall, exhibiting Jacobello del Fiore's "*Winged Lion*" and Antonello da Saliba's "*Christ and Angels*" - wherefrom we pass on into the terrace garden; the Hall of Stuccoes or Priuli Hall, with paintings by Salviati ("*Holy Family*") and Pordenone ("*The Dead Christ*"); and the Hall of the Philosophers - so named

*Doge's Palace.
Titian, "Saint Cristopher" (fresco).*

63

Doge's Palace. G.B. Tiepolo, Venice and Neptune   *Detail of the painting by A. Vicentino*

because numerous paintings of the philosophers once hung there, done by Tintoretto for the Marciana Library. From the balcony of this room the apse of the Basilica can be seen. It is from here, as well, that the doge proceeded down a small stairway straight into the halls of the Senate and the College. Over the doorway there is a fresco by Titian of "*St Christopher*", done in 1523-24.

In the three rooms now used as a Picture Gallery, there are a number of paintings collected from various sources, including: (1st room) "*Christ Mourned*" by Giovanni Bellini, "*Lion Passant*" by Vittore Carpaccio, "*Madonna*" on a gold ground, of the school of Giotto, and "*Madonna and Child*" by Boccaccino. (2nd room) "*St. Jerome*" (triptych), "*Martyrdom of St Juliana*" (triptych), "*Paradise*", "*Inferno*", all by Hieronymus Bosch; "*Inferno*" by Civetta and paintings by the Bassano brothers; and "*Christ Mocked*" by Quentin Metsys; (3rd room) Some paintings by Bassano. Hall of the Squires, with a painting by

Doge's Palace. A. Vicentino, "Arrival of the French king Henry III in Venice"

Gianbattista Tiepolo (1745-1750) showing "*Venice and Neptune*".

With this room your visit to the Ducal Apartment comes to an end. Now you reach the Golden Staircase again and climb up to the rooms on the second floor, going into a Square Anteroom with a painting by Tintoretto of "Doge Priuli with Peace and Justice".

From the Square Anteroom we proceed to the Hall of the Four Doors, built from a drawing by Andrea Palladio after the 1574 fire. The work was carried out under the supervision of the chief architect of the Palace, Giovan Antonio Rusconi. The room occupies the whole width of the Palace from courtyard to canal.

The ceiling panels are richly decorated with frescoes by Tintoretto, symbolising the power of Venice and the cities and regions under her dominion. On the walls we find Titian's painting, "*Doge Grimani Adoring Faith*", Caliari's "*Doge Pasquale Cicogna Receiving Gifts from the Persian Ambassadors*", and Vicentino's "*Henry III of France Arriving in Venice*".

Ducal Palace. G. Caliari. "Doge Marino Grimani receives Gifts from the Persian ambassadors".

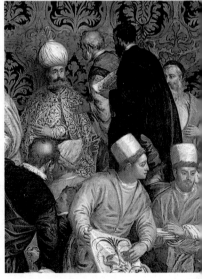

Ducal Palace.
P. Veronese, "Rape of Europe"

Ducal Palace.
G. Caliari. "Doge Marino Grimani receives
Gifts from the Persian ambassadors" (Det.)

Continuing on we come to the **Hall of the Ante-college**, which in the taste of its stucco decorations recalls the Hall of the Four Doors. The statues over the doorway are by Alessandro Vittoria, while the telamons and the frieze of the fireplace, designed by Scamozzi, are by Tiziano Aspetti. The octagonal panel in the ceiling is a work by Paolo Veronese, repainted a number of times.

Doge's Palace. College, ceiling detail

The four canvases on the walls, done by Tintoretto about 1577, show "*Vulcan's Forge*", "*Mercury and the Graces*", "*Pallas Driving away Mars*", and "*The Discovery of Ariadne*". Other works in the same room are "*The Rape of Europa*" by Veronese and "*The Return of Jacob from Canaan*" by Jacopo Bassano.

The **Hall of the College** is one of the most harmonious in its decorations; like the Senate, which is adjacent, it was designed by Andrea Palladio and Giovan Antonio Rusconi, under the supervision of Antonio da Ponte, after the fire in 1574. The ceiling, done between 1577 and 1578 by

Pp. 68/69
Ducal Palace, Antecollege.
J. Tintoretto, "Vulcan's Forge"

Ducal Palace, Antecollege.
J. Tintoretto, "Mercury and the Graces"

Ducal Palace, Antecollege.
J. Tintoretto, "Pallas Driving away Mars"

Ducal Palace, Antecollege.
J. Tintoretto, "Discovery of Ariadne"

Ducal Palace. College, ceiling (detail.)

Ducal Palace. College, ceiling (detail.)

Francesco Bello and Andrea Faentin, frames a number of panels decorated by Paolo Veronese.

In the central panels, "*Mars and Neptune*", "*Faith*", "*Justice and Peace Pay Homage to Venice*"; in the side panels, symbolic figures: "*Faithfulness*", "*Prosperity*", "*Meekness*", "*Simplicity*", and the most celebrated of them all, "*Dialectics*".

On the walls over the stalls: "*Sebastiano Venier after the Battle of Lepanto*" by Paolo Veronese, done in 1578, and other works by Tintoretto, showing the Doges Alvise Mocenigo, Nicolò da Ponte, Francesco Donà and Andrea Gritti, in various attitudes thanking the Virgin and Saints. The stalls and tribunes are the original ones. It was in this room that the highest authorities of the state, i. e. the Doge with his Counsellors, the Sages, and the Heads of the Council of Ten, received the foreign ambassadors, the legates, and noble Venetians on their return from missions abroad.

It was in the **Senate Hall** that one of the most important bodies in the Republic used to meet. This was made up of Senators or "Pregadi", who were so named because the Doge "prayed" them to come in from the nearby Hall of the Four Doors. The ceiling, designed and executed by Cristoforo Sorte (1581 circa), is composed of large panels with highly decorated frames. The paintings in the room were done between 1585 and 1595, during the reign of Pasquale Cicogna.

Doge's Palace. Senate Hall

Doge's Palace. Senate Hall. Detail, central part of ceiling

In the central panel: "*The Triumph of Venice*" by Jacopo Tintoretto; in the ovals at the sides: "*Venus at Vulcan's forge*" by Andrea Vicentino; and "*The Doge Surrounded by Historians and Poets*", by Andrea Vassilacchi, called l'Aliense. The two large clocks on the walls among the paintings help to enrich the decorations.

Among the paintings especially worthy of note are those by Tintoretto and his assistants: "*The Dead Christ*

between *Doge Pietro Lando and Doge Marcantonio Trevisan*", "*Doge Pietro Loredan Praying for the Cessation of the Plague*", and the ones by Jacopo Palma the Younger: "*Venice and Doge Venier Receiving Gifts from the Subject Cities*" and "*Allegory of the League of Cambrai*", with Doge Leonardo Loredan and Venice faced by symbolic figures.

Hall of the Council of Ten. This body was instituted in 1319 after the Bajamonte Tiepolo plot. Although it was formed to deal with a very particular situation, it became an established institution. It attended to matters concerning state security, with wide powers regarding political crimes, and therefore had at its command a secret police force of terrible efficiency. The Tribunal consisted of ten annually elected members and the Doge himself, with six Counsellors. Of the original room furnishings, there remain only the back panels of the semi-

circular tribune against which the seats were arranged. Hidden passageways linked the room to the vertical connections with the internally-related offices, the prison cells, etc.

The ceiling was painted between 1553 and 1554, and the works in the panels are all allegorical scenes by Gianbattista Ponchino, Paolo Veronese and Gianbattista Zelotti. The Hall of the Bussola, named after the wooden porch which masks two

Hall of the Council of Ten. P. Veronese, "Young Woman and Old Man"

Hall of the Council of Ten

doors, one leading to the Leads and the other to the Wells. This room functioned as a vestibule or waiting room for condemned or accused people while they waited to enter the tribunal. The only complete and undamaged Lion's mouth remaining is set in one wall: this served for depositing accusations. We may observe that the small shutter has two locks; in fact, it could by opened only by the two magistrates in charge - together, and each with his own key.

G.B. Ponchino, "Mercury and Minerva" (detail.)

P. Veronese,
"Juno offers Venice the Ducal Horn"

Hall of the Bussola

Armoury. A Hall

Armoury. The arms belonging to the Council of Ten from the 15th century on were stored here and kept in efficient condition in case of emergency. They are mostly of kinds typical at the time, while a few have a purely decorative interest and were used only for parades and particular ceremonies.

Among the sidearms there are single and two-hand swords, broadswords, daggers, axes. Staff weapons: halberds, falchions, pikes, billhooks, ranseurs. Armour: the armour belonging to the condottiere Erasmo da Narni, called Gattamelata, is famous, as is the equestrian suit belonging to Henry IV of France, a gift from the King to the Republic in 1603; not to mention an incomplete jousting suit by the Milanese Missaglia.

Parts of suits of armour: basinets, brigandines, burgonets, casques, cuirasses, morions, shields, bucklers, pavise shields, bows, arrows, and crossbows, including the one which, as history recounts, the Signor Da Carrara used to amuse himself with by shooting at passers-by from his window.

Firearms: harquebuses, wheel-lock pistols, sawed-off shotguns. Miscellaneous weapons: for throwing or firing, or in the form of maces, swords or crossbows.

Among the fines pieces there is a dog-faced basinet of Italian 15th-century workmanship, a bronze culverin with beautiful floral relief work, Italian craft works of the early 16th century attributed to Alberghetti, a twenty-barrelled

Venetian-style helmet without crest (15th cent)
Morion with crest
Sallet helmet
Rapier

harquebus signed by G.M. Bergamin; a five-chamber revolver-action stone-projector; various instruments of torture, and a chastity belt which the 1548 inventory describes as iron trousers belonging to the wife of the Lord of Padua.

We come out of the Armoury and go down the Censors' Stairway to the floor of the great halls: the Hall of the Great Council and the Hall of the Scrutiny. We pass into the Liagò, i. e. the vestibule of the Hall of the Great Council, brightly-lit due to its pointed arched openings overlooking the Basin of Saint Mark; on the left side we find the Hall of the Quarantia Civil Vecchia, premises for a magistracy consisting of forty members who heard civil cases; then the Hall of the Armoury or Hall of Guariento. This last name was given the room because it was used to store the fragments of the great fresco by the Paduan artist Guariento, "*The Coronation of the Virgin*", which once decorated one of the smaller walls of the Hall of the Great Council. The work was executed between 1365 and 1367, but was very badly damaged in the 1577 fire, and was left, forgotten, beneath Tintoretto's huge canvas rediscovered and "strappato" in 1903.

Hall of the Great Council. This is the largest hall in the whole Doge's Palace: it measures 54 by 25 metres and is 12 metres high. It was here that the Great Council, the highest body of the State, used to meet. At first its members numbered 300, and later increased to 1600.

The first decorations of the "ship's keel"- shaped ceiling were painted by Gentile da Fabriano, Pisanello, Alvise Vivarini, Giovanni Bellini, Vittore Carpaccio, Titian, Pordenone, Veronese and Tintoretto, and were completely destroyed by fire. This was an immense loss to the artistic heritage of Venice and the world. The fire broke out during the night, in 1577, somewhere near the Porta della Carta, and spread as far as this point.

Restoration of the great hall's interior proceeded rapidly between 1578 and 1595, during the reigns of Nicolò da Ponte and Pasquale Cicogna. Of all the painters whose works had been destroyed in the fire, only Veronese and Tintoretto took part in its redecoration.

The new series of paintings, no longer frescoes but canvases, for the most part deal with the subjects of the previous ones. Their distribution was planned by the monk Gerolamo Bardi and the historian Francesco Sansovino. The ceiling, richly decorated in carved and gilded cornices, was executed according to a design by Cristoforo Sorte.

The panel images represent the glorification of the Republic and events such as battles and the conquest of the mainland territories. From the entrance the central section shows: "*The Triumph of Venice among the Gods of Mount Olym-*

Views of the Hall of the Great Council

pus", by Paolo Veronese, "*Doge Da Ponte Receiving an Olive Branch from Venice*", by Tintoretto, and "*Venice Crowned by Victory Welcomes the Subject Provinces*", by Palma the Younger. On the lateral strips are Venetian victories in the Orient and the Veneto, against the Turks and the Milanese: paintings by Tintoretto, Veronese, Palma and Da Ponte.

On the end wall above the tribunal is the huge canvas by Jacopo Tintoretto, "*The Coronation of the Virgin*" (1590),

showing hundreds of human figures in successive ranks according to their various grades of beatitude - angels, saints and blessed souls - all circling round the central point above formed by the Virgin kneeling before the Saviour, whose figure radiates divine light. On the walls there are two historical cycles. To the right, The Struggle between Frederick Barbarossa and Alexander III, or between the Empire and Papacy, illustrating the Venetian Republic's role as mediator in the figure of Doge Sebastiano Ziani (only partly confirmed by history). There are twelve paintings showing the various events in this struggle, by the following artists in the order presented: B. and C. Caliari, author of the first two paintings, L. Bassano, Tintoretto and assistants, F. Bassano, P. Dei Franceschi, A. Vicentino, Palma the Younger, F. Zuccari, G. Gamberato, G. Del Moro. On the left side is the History of the Fourth Crusade (1201-1204). It consists of a series of eight paintings: from the taking of the oath in the Basilica of Saint

P. Veronese, "Apotheosis of Venice". Above: detail

F. Bassano, the "Doge Sets Sail against Barbarossa"

J. Tintoretto, "Coronation of the Virgin"

Battle of Salvore (detail)
John Le Clerc, The Captains Take Oath in Saint Mark's Basilica (detail.)

Mark, to the conquest of Constantinople, and the coronation of King Baldwin. The painters, in order of sequence: G. Saraceni and G. Leclerc, A. Vicentino, D. Tintoretto, A. Vicentino, Palma the Younger, D. Tintoretto, A. Vicentino, l'Aliense.

On the wall facing the throne, in the middle between the windows, there is a work by Veronese showing "*Doge Contarini Returning to Venice after Defeating the Genoese at Chioggia*" (1379).

Between the ceiling and the paintings there is a long frieze that runs all round the room, with portraits of the Doges, nearly all by Domenico Tintoret-

to and collaborators. In the panel dedicated to Marin Faliero there is a black cloth with the words "Hic est locus Marini Falethri, decapitati pro criminibus". Marin Faliero was in fact decapitated in 1355, after the failure of his plot against the Venetian Republic. From the middle balcony, a work done in the early 15th century by the Dalle Masegne, we can enjoy a view of the spacious Basin with the islands of San Giorgio and Giudecca, while to the right is the Punta della Dogana and the Salute Church. To the left is the Riva degli Schiavoni stretching as far as Sant'Elena.

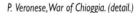

P. Veronese, War of Chioggia. (detail.)

The **Hall of Scrutiny** was badly damaged in the same fire that destroyed the decoration in the Hall of the Great Council, but it was quickly restored.

This room, used as a public library before the Marciana Library was built, was later the site where votes were counted up, during election in the Hall of the Great Council of the doge and other high officials. On the end wall, connected with the Foscara Staircase, which leads to the loggias and the inner courtyard, a monument or triumphal arch was built in honour of Francesco Morosini,

A. Tirali, Triumphal Arch

called il Peloponnesiaco to celebrate his victories over the Turks in Morea and the Peloponnesian Peninsula. The design is by Antonio Gaspari, and the paintings of allegorical subjects are by Gregorio Lazzarini. On the right-hand wall three paintings recall glorious war episodes and Venetian victories over the Hungarians and Turks: "The Venetians Conquer the Hungarians and Capture Zara" by Jacopo Tintoretto, "The Battle of Lepanto" by Andrea Vicentino, "The Venetians Conquer the Turks at the Dardanelles" by Pietro Liberi.

Antonio Vassillacchi, Conquest of Tyre (detail.)

Hall of Scrutiny

Gregorio Lazzarini, "Doge Morosinioffers reconquered Morea to Venice (detail)

From these rooms we go straight to the **Bridge of Sighs**: the bridge links the Ducal Palace with the New Prisons beyond the Canal. The bridge was built at the beginning of the 17th century form a design by Antonio Contin. The name is an invention of Romantic literature; while sighing over its beauty, the Romantics imagined the anguished sighs of condemned prisoners passing over it, on their way to the dungeons.

The New Prisons, on the other side of the canal, were built in three successive periods from 1566 to the early 17th century. The part facing the Riva degli Schiavoni, and the wing on the Calle degli Albanesi, were built to a design by Antonio da Ponte, who created his building round the courtyard, grafting it onto the re-existing

blocks of eight, served by an external passageway. These belong to the oldest part of the building.

Bridge of Sighs

Marble grate on the Bridge of Sighs.

Returning to the Ducal Palace by way of the second passage in the Bridge, we come into the Avogaria, which consists of a series of rooms, once the premises of a number of administrative bodies: the Hall of the Censors, the Hall of the Notaries, the Hall of the Scrigno (where the noble family registers were kept), the Hall of the Attorneys of Marine Supplies, the Hall of the Great Seal. There are a number of paintings here, mostly portraits of magistrates, by Domenico Tintoretto, Leandro Bassano, Sebastiano Bombelli and Filippo Zaniberti.

To conclude our tour we can visit the Pozzi (wells), the only prisons left inside the palace itself. They were particularly unhealthy owing to their position on the ground floor and their dampness. One of them still has its original wainscoting and a wooden bench which served as a bed for the prisoner.

Cell in the Palace Prisons
Torture room

Palace Prisons beyond the canal, facing St. Mark's Basin

2 ITINERARY

GRAND CANAL

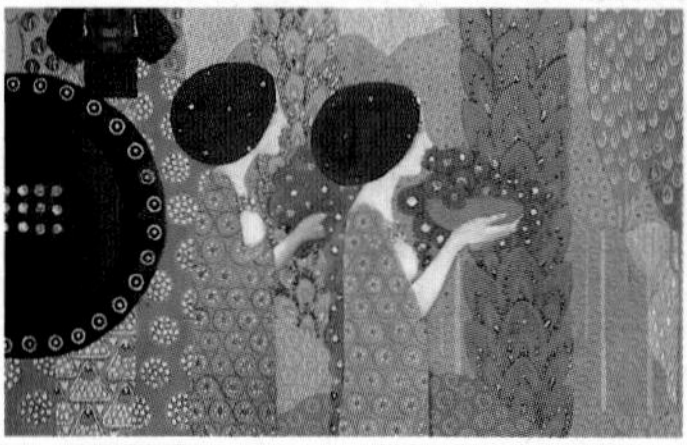

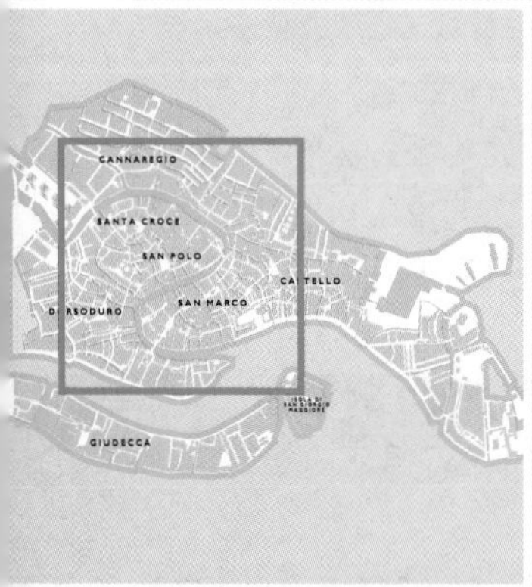
CANNAREGIO
SANTA CROCE
SAN POLO
SAN MARCO
GIUDECCA

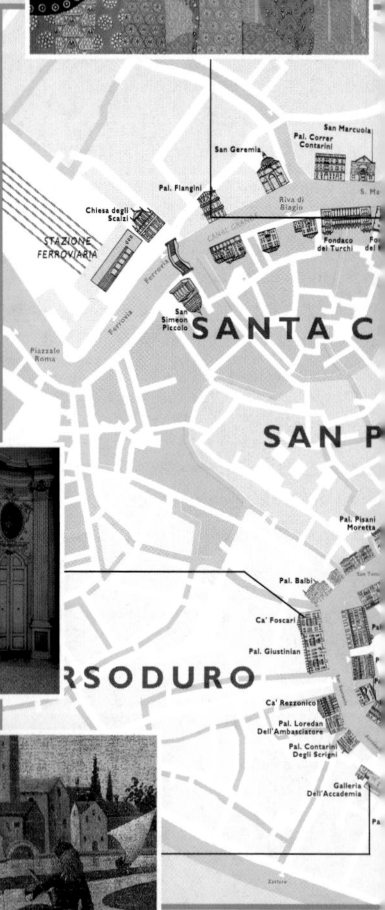
San Marcuola
Pal. Correr Contarini
San Geremia
Pal. Flangini
Riva di Biagio
Chiesa degli Scalzi
STAZIONE FERROVIARIA
Fondaco dei Turchi
Ferrovia
San Simeon Piccolo
Piazzale Roma
Pal. Pisani Moretta
Pal. Balbi
Ca' Foscari
Pal. Giustinian
Ca' Rezzonico
Pal. Loredan Dell'Ambasciatore
Pal. Contarini Degli Scrigni
Galleria Dell'Accademia
Zattere

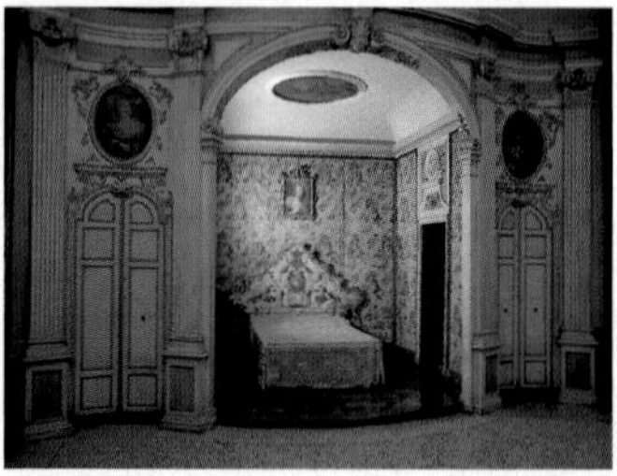

Cà Rezzonico. The Alcove

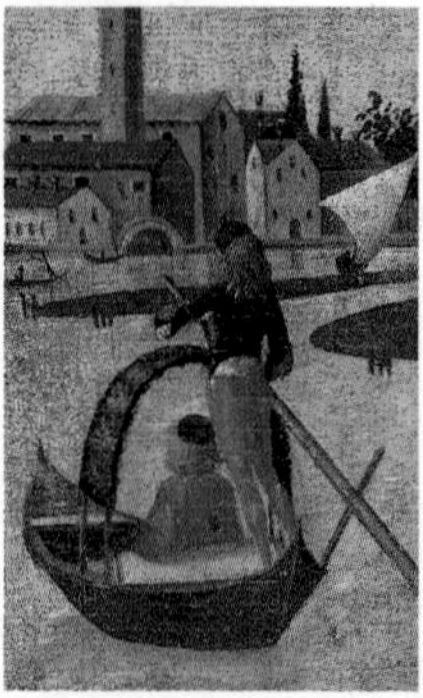

Accademia Galleries.
Vittore Carpaccio,
"St. Ursula Cycle" (detail.)

Cà Pesaro. Modern Art Museum.
Vittorio Zecchin, Thousand and One Nights (detail.)

Cà d'Oro façade.
Window detail

Venier Dei Leoni Palace

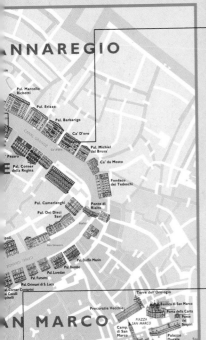

NNAREGIO

Pal. Marcello
Richetti
Pal. Erizzo
Pal. Barbarigo
Ca' D'oro
Pal. Michiel
dal Brusa'
Pesaro
Ca' da Mosto
Pal. Corner
della Regina
Fondaco
dei Tedeschi
Pal. Camerlenghi
Ponte di
Rialto
Pal. Dei Dieci
Savi
oli
Pal. Dolfin Manin
Pal. Bembo
Pal. Farsetti
Pal. Loredan
al. Corner Contarini
Pal. Grimani di S. Luca
Corell
pinell

Torre dell'Orologio
Basilica di San Marco
Procuratie Vecchie
Porta della Carta
Ponte
dei
Sospiri

AN MARCO

PIAZZA
SAN MARCO
Camp.
di San
Marco
Palazzo
Ducale
Pal. Contarini
Fasan
Pal. Giustinian
baro
Lib. Marciana
Pal. Hotel
Gritti
Pal. Barozzi
Emo
Zecca
Corner
Grande

Pal.
Venier
dei Leoni
Coll.
Guggenheim
Pal.
Dario
Punta della
Dogana
Santa Maria
della Salute
Abbazia
di San
Gregorio

Basilica of Santa Maria
della Salute

St. Mark's Basin

In front of us opens Saint Mark's Basin with the Mint (Zecca) on the right and the Ducal Palace on the left, followed by the long curved shore of the Riva degli Schiavoni leading as far as the island of Sant'Elena, which was at one time the site of numberous shipyards. Facing us is **Saint George**, in ancient times called the Island of Cypresses for the cypress trees growing there. In 982 it was granted to Giovanni Morosini by the Republic, and he founded a Benedictine monastery there. As a result of special privileg-

St. Mark's Basin

es and bequests received from emperors, popes and doges, in particular from Sebastiano Ziani (buried there in 1178), it was continually enriched in such a way as to soon become a religious and cultural centre of European fame. The buildings rising here were all destroyed in the earthquake of 1223, and reconstructed with the assistance of Doge Pietro Ziani, who died on this peaceful island in 1229. From the first half of the 15th century on, work continued steadily until the early years of the 17th century. Cosimo Lord of

Florence, while exiled in Padua, visited Venice and lived on this island for a brief period. The architect Michelozzo Michelozzi, whom Cosimo had brought with him, constructed the Library, the first example in Venice of Renaissance architecture; unfortunately it was later pulled down, The Dormitory (known as the Manica Lunga or Long Sleeve) is a fascinating building, especially in the interior, with its cells in the two wings and a central corridor 128 metres long by Giovanni Buora. The Laurel Cloister, built on Giovanni Buora's plans, was finished by his son Andrea. On the other sides the guests' quarters and the Abbot's residence

Cypress Cloister

were built. The Chapter House also forms part of the sixteenth-century complex of buildings. From 1559 on, Palladio worked on the island. He built the Refectory between 1559 and 1563; the Church of Saint George with its square begun in 1579 and finished around 1610; the Cypress Cloister between 1579 and 1614. After the death of Palladio (1580) the buildings were completed by other architects. In the 17th century the last constructions were executed by Longhena, notably the Grand Stairway in the first cloister (1641-1643), the Abbots' Apartments overlooking Saint Mark's Basin and the Library (1641 1671).

Saint Georges island

GRAND CANAL
LEFT BANK

Dogana da Mar (maritime Customs house), built around 1677 by the architect Giuseppe Benoni. The part forming the point is built in the form of a tower surmounted by a gilded globe symbolising Fortune. Here, from the 14th century on, cargoes were unloaded and customs duties on them were paid.

The **Seminary**, by Longhena, a seventeenth-century building on the site of the former Monastery of the Trinity.

Church of the Salute by Longhena, erected between 1631 and 1687 (page 120).

Dario Palace built about 1487 for Giovanni Dario, secretary to the Republic in Constantinople, on plans by Pietro Lombardo. The façade is distinctive not only for its oblique angle due to the subsidence of its foundations, but for the great attention given to detail: the decorations and framings of polychrome marbles, both in the windowed area and in the wall panels themselves.

Sea Customs House

Church of La Salute

Dario Palace

Venier Dei Leoni Palace. The intention of the patrons and the architect, Lorenzo Boschetti, who conceived it around 1749, was to erect an edifice of colossal size. It was interrupted at the first-floor level for lack of funds due to the proprietors' reversals of fortune. At present it houses the Peggy Guggenheim Modern Art Gallery.

Peggy Guggenheim (1898-1979) formed the most important part of her collection with the intention of founding a contemporary art museum, between 1938 and 1947, in London, Paris and New York. In 1942, in New York she opened the Art of This Century gallery-museum, where she exhibited her collection of avant-garde European artists,

View of the Grand Canal with Venier Dei Leoni Palace

The **Peggy Guggenheim Collection** is a modern art museum housing numerous painting masterworks belonging to the avant-garde of the early 20th century. Cubism, European abstract art, surrealism and abstract expressionism are well represented.

In the new wing of the museum, we find the museum shop and museum café (open during visiting hours). In addition, temporary exhibitions are held according to a varied calendar.

and organised various exhibitions dedicated to young American artists such as Robert Motherwell, Mark Rothko, Clyfford Still and Jackson Pollock. The collection was first shown in Europe at the Venice Biennale in 1948. The following year Peggy Guggenheim purchased the unfinished palazzo Venier Dei Leoni (second half of the 18th century) and immediately chose it as her house, placing in its rooms the masterpieces collected up to that time, and later opening it to the public as a museum. Assembled

Venier Dei Leoni Palace, seat of Peggy Guggenheim Collection The Solomon R. Guggenheim Foundation

in accordance with the advice of artists and critics such as Marcel Duchamp and Herbert Read, and her second husband, Max Ernst, it is one of the world's most important collections of its kind. In 1976, Peggy Guggenheim left the palace and collection to the Solomon R. Guggenheim foundation, which now acts as their curator, in cooperation with the other Guggenheim Museums in New York, Bilbao and Berlin. The entry hall to the palazzo displays highly important works by Picasso "*On the Beach*", "*Study*", as well as a mobile by Alexander Calder. From the entryway one can pass to the terrace overlooking the Grand Canal, with Marino Marini's sculpture, "*Angel of the City*". On re-entering the palazzo we find that the collection continues, with important cubist masterpieces by Picasso "*Poet*", Braque "*Clarinet*", Léger, Duchamp, Gris, Gleizes, Metzinger and Delaunay. Early contemporary painting in Italy is represented by the Futurists (Boccioni, Balla, Severini) and Giorgio de Chirico. European abstract art is represented in works by Kupka, Kandinsky "*Landscape with Red Patches*", "*White Cross*", Mondrian, Van Doesburg, Malevich, Pevsner, Lissitzky and Hélion. In addition, we find works by Arp, Picabia, Schwitters and Ernst, which are linked to the Dada movement, while the fantastic elements present in works by Chagall "*Rain*" and Klee "*Magic Garden*" connect these artists to surrealism well represented by Ernst "*Dressing of the Bride*", "*Antipope*", Miro' "*Dutch Interior II*", "*Woman Sitting II*", Magritte "*Empire of Light*", Delvaux, Dali' and Tanguy, as well as others. The help which Peggy Guggenheim offered to young American artists in the 40s is reflected in the presence of Jackson Pollock "*Moon Woman*", "*Alchemy*", in early works by Motherwell, Rothko, Baziotes and Still, and in a large painting by Gorky. The collection also includes

Kazimir Malevich, "Untitled"

important sculptures: two bronzes by Brancusi "*Maiastra*", "*Bird in Space*", and works by Giacometti "*Woman Walking*", "*Woman with Cut Throat*". Peggy Guggenheim's bedhead, created by Alexander Calder, is a unique work. Since September 1997, thanks to a long-term loan granted by the heirs, the museum has also housed in the so-called "barchessa" twenty-six works from the Gianni Mattioli collection, containing some of the most important masterpieces of Italian Futurism: Boccioni's "*Matter and Dynamism of a Cyclist*", Carrà's "*Interventionist Demon-*

stration", Russolo's "*Solidity of Fog*"; plus works by Balla, Severini, Depero, Rosai, Soffici, Sironi. Among the works exhibited we can also find paintings by the young Morandi and Modigliani. The Nasher Sculpture Garden of the Peggy Guggenheim Collection displays sculptures from the Raymond and Patsy Nasher Sculpture Collection of Dallas, Texas, besides works from the museum's permanent collection. Works presently shown include sculptures by Ernst, Giacometti, Moore, Arp, Richier, Merz, Di Suvero, Morris, Duchamp-Villon, Minguzzi and Gilardi.

Contarini-Fasan Palace, a small building rich with architectural and decorative elements in flamboyant Gothic style (circa 1475). The designs on the main-floor balconies are highly interesting.

Contarini Fasan Palace

Flangini-Fini Palace of the late 17th century, attributed to Alessandro Tremignon. The Fini family also commissioned the façade of the church of San Moisé.

Gritti Palace, now a hotel, is a pointed-arched Gothic building of the 14th century, whose façade was once decorated with frescoes by Giorgione. Campo S. Maria del Giglio, with the church of this name boldly foreshortened in the background.

Corner Della Ca' Grande Palace, now the seat of the Prefecture of Venice. The building was commissioned by Jaco-

po Corner o between 1532 and 1561 on plans by Jacopo Sansovino. The façade is contained within the geometrical figure of a square subdivided into three horizontal bands, highlighted by the rusticated ground floor from which open the three large portals of the atrium, by the string-courses and the boldly-projecting balconies. There is a square courtyard in the rear enclosed within the main body of the building.

Gritti Palace

Corner Della Ca' Grande Palace

Contarini Dal Zaffo Palace, built towards the end of the 15th century and brought to completion in the early 16th century. Critics are uncertain whether to attribute the palace to Coducci or to Lombardo, for while the general composition recalls the former, the style and taste exhibited by the polychrome marble decoration is more usual in the latter.

Contarini Dal Zaffo Palace

Galleries of the Academy (page 124)

Contarini Dagli Scrigni Palaces. The first was planned in about 1610 by Vincenzo Scamozzi as an enlargement of the second building, and the artist's attempt to maintain the same levels in his subdivision of the floors was detrimental to the proportions of the building. The second, in fifteenth-century Gothic style, was restructured by Francesco Smeraldi in the 17th century.

Loredan Palace, known as dell'Ambasciatore since in the 17th century it was the seat of the Roman ambassadors to the Republic. The building is in fifteenth-century Gothic style, and has typical quatrefoils or grouped lancet windows.

Moro Palace (16th century).

Contarini Dagli Scrigni Palace

Grassi Palace

Barbaro Palaces. The first belongs to the 17th century; the second is Gothic (14th-15th century) and was for a time the home of Isabella d'Este, wife of the Marquis of Mantua.

Franchetti Palace (15th cent).

Giustinian-Lolin Palace. One of Longhena's first works, carried out in about 1632, it represents the restructuring of an earlier fourteenth-century Gothic building. The elongated windows were necessitated by the preceding architectural context.

Grassi Palace has its main façade overlooking the Grand Canal and a side façade on Campo San Samuele, where the ancient twelfth-century bell-tower and the church of the same name rise. The Grassi family commissioned this sumptuous residence in 1748, entrusting the building to Giorgio Massari, who brought it to completion towards 1776.

Contarini Dalle Figure Palace, so named because of the two carya-

Loredan Dell'Ambasciatore Palace

tids which support the balcony, is a Renaissance structure of the early 16th century attributed to Scarpagnino. The layout of the façade is clearly of Lombard origin.

Contarini Dalle Figure Palace

Rezzonico Palace

Ca' Rezzonico (page 168). Built by B. Longhena in the mid 17th century and finished in 1745 by Giorgio Massari, it is now the seat of a Museum of the Venetian Eighteenth Century.

Giustinian Palaces and Foscari Palace. The two Giustinian buildings are identical in size and mirror one another. The central portal corresponds to the calle which divides them. The later one, at the canal intersection, was built about 1452 for Doge Foscari, though when he died in 1457 the palace was not yet finished. It is one of the largest palaces on the Grand Canal, with two very high main floors and a central hall with a long row of spacious grouped windows. In the background is the wall surrounding the

Giustinian Palaces

vast courtyards where a monumental external staircase once led to the upper floors. This palace and the two Giustinian Palaces are attributed to the architects Giovanni and Bartolomeo Bon. The three buildings now house the University, known as Ca' Foscari.

Foscari Palace

Balbi Palace

Balbi Palace rises at the bend where Rio Foscari joins the Grand Canal. This palace was built between 1582 and 1590, apparently after plans by Alessandro Vittoria. The architectural elements of the façade show how sixteenth-century taste was evolving constantly towards greater freedom and plasticity, thus heralding the Baroque.

Mocenigo Palaces. The Mocenigo family owned a series of Gothic buildings. In the 17th century the interior of the first building, called Casa Vecchia, was restructured, and its façade completely renovated. About 1580 the reconstruction of the second building known as the Ca' Nova was begun, mirroring the manner in which new forms were evolving from Sansovino's and Palladio's Renaissance experiments. These two buildings were subsequently joined by twin palaces. In 1592 Giordano Bruno was a guest in the second palace, until his host denounced him to the Inquisitions. Anne, Countess of Shrewsbury also lived here. Her relationship with the patrician, Antonio Fos-

Mocenigo Palace. Casa Nova

carini, caused him to be accused of high treason and he was put to death.

Garzoni Palace, an impressive Gothic building of the 15th century with two main floors, is at present in a precarious state of repair and is now abandoned.

Corner-Spinelli Palace. The building is characterised by the same architectural and structural elements mentioned in the Vendramin-Calergi Palace, and both bear the stamp of the architect, Mauro Coducci. The edifice dates from the late 15th to the early 16th century. Around 1542 the interior was partially rearranged by Michele Sanmicheli.

The Mocenigo Palaces

Corner-Spinelli Palace

Benzon Palace. Famous for its receptions and literary salons frequented by such famous writers and artists as Canova, Lord Byron, Foscolo, Pindemonte and others between the late 18th and early 19th century.

Pisani-Moretta Palace. The Gothic style is finely expressed in this building with its row of six quatrefoil windows and designs differing between the first and second floors. The mid fifteenth-century construction was later rear-

Corner Dei Cavalli Palace

ranged with the addition of a grand three-flight stairway at the head of the central hall.

Barbarigo Della Terrazza Palace constructed around 1568 is most probably attributabie to plans by Bernardino Contin. Its terrace garden above the ground floor indicates that the building was interrupted.

Grimani Palace. The present building with its small rear courtyard was built in the 16th century on the site of an ancient Byzantine construction. It is another example of the triple partitioned façade, decorated with polychrome marbles in the manner of the school of the Lombardos.

Bernardo Palace. In Gothic style, it was built around 1442. The external stairway in the courtyard is particularly striking.

Pisani Moretta Palace

Grimani Marcello Palace

Corner-Contarini Dai Cavalli Palace, so named from the two horses in the crest of the armorial bearings on the façade. The flamboyant Gothic building dates back to the mid 15th century.

Grimani Palace. At the intersection with the San Luca Canal, it was built by Michele Sanmicheli during the first half of the 16th century. On the death of the architect in 1559 the building was not yet finished. The patron's desire to invest his new residence with an impressive monumentality is evident, and the artist succeeded well in the task: not only in the massiveness of its volume, but also in the grandiose arches on the levels above the ground floor, in the deep-colonnaded atrium on the ground floor and the powerful projecting string-courses.

Ca' Dandolo-Farsetti and Ca' Loredan-Corner: the two palaces separated by a calle date back to the late twelfth-to-early 13th century.

Grimani Palace

Farsetti and Loredan Palaces

Here, developed in a stately manner, are the traditional motifs of the Byzantine casa-fondaco, with a portico at ground level and loggia on the main floor, in this case running the whole length of the façade. Both buildings underwent numerous reconstruction efforts and during the 16th century were raised two storeys higher, enlarged, and internally transformed. They now house the offices of the town hall.

Tiepolo-Papadopoli Palace

Tiepolo-Papadopoli Palace, erected towards the middle of the 16th century by Guglielmo dei Grigi. The building presents a massive effect of volume. The façade with the central portal and the three-bay centre at each floor is subdivided by projecting string-courses.

A series of Byzantine structures follows, partly restored and in varying degrees stripped of their true character:

the two Donà Palaces, Businello Palace and Barzizza Palace. They remain as evidence of the building activity during the 12th-13th centuries. This was already a densely-populated area owing to the proximity of the Rialto market.

Ten Sages Palace. The minor façade overlooks the Grand Canal while the main front opens along the interior, reaching as far as Ruga Vecchia di San Giovanni Elemosinario. It was constructed after the great fire of 1514, between 1520 and 1522, after plans by Antonio Scarpagnino.

RIALTO BRIDGE

The two banks have been spanned since time immemorial, first by a bridge of boats and later by a wooden drawbridge on pilings. After much consideration, and after the commissioning of various projects among which the best known remains Palladio's, it was not until 1588 that the construction of a stone bridge designed by Antonio da Ponte and his nephew Antonio Contin was decided upon. In 1591 the bridge already included the upper part, destined to house a series of shops.

Rialto Bridge

Rialto Bridge

Fondaco Dei Tedeschi

German Merchants's Warehouse (Fondaco Dei Tedeschi). This building, like the Turkish Merchants', was rented out to a foreign community, namely the Germans, who were very numerous and active in Venice. On a square ground-plan with an internal courtyard graced by loggias, it was reconstructed after a fire and finished towards 1508 by Giorgio Spavento and Scarpagnino. The façade once bore frescoes by Giorgione (see fragments at the Academy Galleries). A nineteenth-century restoration partly modified the building's façade, demolishing the two lateral towers.

Civran Palace, a reconstruction of an earlier Byzantine palace by Giorgio Massari between 1715 and 1720.

Ca' Da Mosto. Dating back to the 12th-13th centuries and marred by the seventeenth-century addition to the upper part, in its proportions it clearly reveals the aspect of a Byzantine house-warehouse. The ground-floor portico leads to the interior warehouse, while the central window group and separate side windows on the first floor correspond to the dwelling's central salon and the side rooms opening off it. From the 16th century onwards this building was one of the city's most renowned and exclusive hotels, the Albergo del Leon Bianco (White Lion Hotel). Here, towards the end of the 18th century, Emperor Joseph II and the Northern counts took lodgings. The Republic held extraordinary banquets in their honour in Saint Mark's Square, where intricate scaffolds were erected for jousts and bull-baiting.

Michiel Dalle Colonne Palace, thus called from the ground-floor portico still bearing the stamp of its Byzantine origins despite later restructuring of the entire façade by Giuseppe Sardi in the last half of the 17th century.

Ca' Da Mosto
Michiel Dalle Colonne Palace

Camerlenghi Palace (Palace of the Public Treasury). The seat of an important Venetian magistracy concerned with State finances, and of other, less important departments of the magistracy, on the ground floor of which were debtors' prisons. On the site of the ancient merchants' loggia, this building was erected between 1525 and 1528, perhaps after

Camerlenghi Palace with Rialto Bridge

Camerlenghi Palace

plans by Guglielmo dei Grigi, a native of Bergamo. The free-standing building, contrary to most Venetian palaces, is finished and decorated to the same extent on all sides. It is a notable example of Renaissance architecture in Venice.

Corner Della Regina Palace. In 1724 Domenico Rossi began the construction on the area of a pre-existing palace belonging to the branch of the Cornaro family known as della Regina (of the Queen), since it was descended from Caterina Cornaro, Queen of Cyprus, who was born her in 1454. Isolated between two narrow lanes, or calli, it presents a very narrow façade, soaring vertically, where seventeenth-century stylistic elements common to the Pesaro and Rezzonico palaces are combined with the already neo-classical motifs of Tirali and Scalfarotto.

Pesaro Palace

Corner Della Regina Palace

Pesaro Palace, now the International Modern Art Gallery and Oriental Museum. On the area previously occupied by three Gothic buildings, Longhena raised one of the Grand Canal's most powerful structures. In 1676 work began in the courtyard area, proceeding as far as the canal façade and the first floor. Building ceased on the death of Longhena in 1682, and was resumed in 1710 by Antonio Gaspari, who completed it with the second floor following the original design by Longhena, though the side on the Rio is Gaspari's. The edifice is one of he most important examples of Venetian Baroque civil architecture, and one of the most complete expressions of the artist's genius.

Ca' D'Oro (Golden House). In the first decades of the 15th century (the building was finished around 1434), Marino Contarini commissioned this precious "golden" house, so named for its brilliant gildings and the polychrome tones of the façade. It was constructed by Matteo Raverti with the aid of Lombard artisans and the brothers Giovanni and Bartolomeo Bon. While the structural elements

Ca' D'Oro. Detail

of the portico recall those of the Byzantine palaces, the two loggias of the upper floor represent the most fantastic expression of Venetian flamboyant Gothic. The building now houses an Art Gallery. (see p. 156).

Gussoni-Grimani Palace built in the 16th century and attributed to Michele Sanmicheli. At one time the façade was decorated with frescoes by Tintoretto.

Ca' D'Oro

Vendramin Calergi Palace

Ca' Vendramin-Calergi. Between the 15th and 16th centuries Mauro Coducci was engaged by the Loredan family to start on his scheme of this palace, which is one of the most significant examples of Venetian Renaissance architecture. Of particular note are the grouped twin lights joined by a single arch which Coducci designed for this and other buildings.

The Cannaregio Canal with the Ponte delle Guglie in the distance, and to the left side the Labia Palace.

Labia Palace, a construction of the mid 18th century by the architect A. Tremignon. Inside are famous frescoes by G. B. Tiepolo. At present the palace houses the Venetian headquarters of RAI-TV (Italian Radio and Television).

Church of San Geremia, whose apse area and lateral façade may be glimpsed at from here, dates back to the 11th century, and assumed its present form in the second half of the 18th century, after plans by C. Corbellini.

Flangini Palace, seventeenth-century architecture by G. Sardi.

Labia Palace and the Church of San Geremia

Campo and Church of San Stae, restructured completely in 1678 by Giovanni Grassi. After a competition held by the Republic and won by Domenico Rossi, it was completed with a new façade by the artist in 1709.

Belloni-Battagia Palace. While restructuring an earlier Gothic building, toward the middle of the 17th century the architect Baldassare Longhena renovated this palace on the inside and rebuilt it with a new façade. In 1663, the palace was probably complete. The artist's hand is revealed in the architectural motifs: broken pediments, enormous escutcheons, smooth ashlars. The main floor is underscored by fine balconies, while a dentilled band, topped with pediments, limits the upper part.

Fondaco del Megio divided from the Warehouse of the Turks by a canal. The Republic had this building constructed in the 15th century for use as a public granary.

Warehouse of the Turkish Merchants, erected in the mid 13th century by Giacomo Palmieri. It was acquired by the Republic for the Marquis of Ferrara. Emperor John Palaeologus of Byzantium stayed there in 1438, and Alfonso d'Este of Ferrara in 1562. In the end, the Republic rented it out to the Turkish community, who used it as a dwelling and storehouse; it became one of the city's most attractive house-warehouses. Reduced to a disastrous state of repair, it was reconstructed in the middle of the 19th century. One cannot speak of restoration, for its whole aspect was then totally falsified.

Belloni-Battagia Palace

Fondaco del Megio

Church of San Simeon Piccolo, constructed between 1718 and 1738 by the architect G. Scalfarotto. The large green dome stands out; the architect must certainly have been inspired by Longhena's dome at the church of La Salute.

Piazzale Roma.

Church of San Simeon Piccolo

Scalzi Church

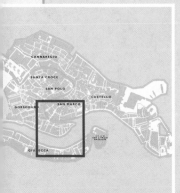

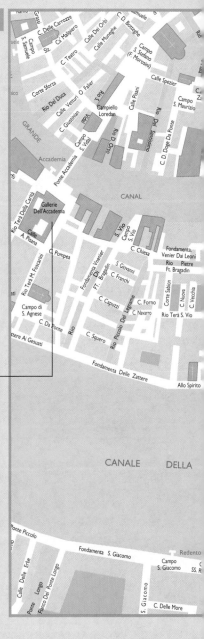

Accademia Galleries.
Carpaccio, St. Ursola Cycle (detail)

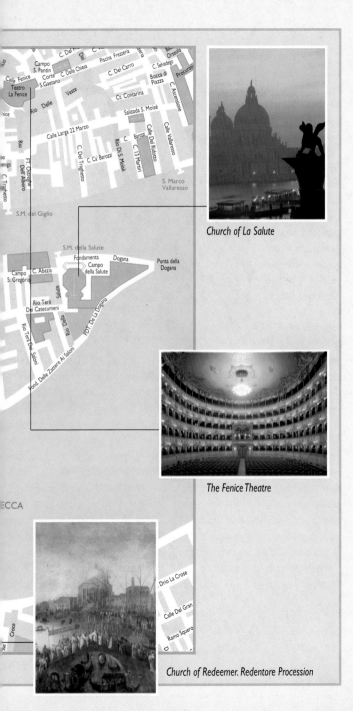

Church of La Salute

The Fenice Theatre

Church of Redeemer. Redentore Procession

After leaving from the landing-stage of San Marco one disembarks directly in front of the **Church of the Salute**. Built by Longhena between 1631 and 1681, it was erected by initiative of the Republic and dedicated to the Holy Virgin in gratitude for the cessation of the plague which had reaped a tragic number of victims in the city. The interior is on a central octagonal plan along whose sides runs an ambulatory. The six chapels open off it. On the axis of the main entrance we find the presbytery. The composite piers of the interior support the drum on which the large dome rises, while a second and smaller cupola is placed above the presbytery and is flanked by two small belfries. Outside, large volutes or scrolls buttress the large cupola, while the façades are decorated with pilasters and tympana.

Inside the church are three important altar-pieces by Luca Giordano, the "Assumption", the "Nativity", and the "Presentation of the Virgin". The main altar was designed by Longhena, the sculptures executed by Giusto La Corte. Above the altar is the image of the Virgin, an icon of the Greco-Byzantine school, brought to Venice in 1672 by Francesco Morosini from the Church of St. Titus in Candia (Crete). Other important paintings in the Salute include works by Pietro Liberi and Alessandro Varotari, and the great canvas "Marriage at Cana" painted by Tintoretto in 1551 (formerly in the suppressed Monastery of the Crociferi). Other paintings are by J. Palma the Younger, Marco Basaiti, and finally eight tondos with heads of the Evangelists and Fathers of the Church, by Titian, as well as his "Sacrifice of Abraham", "David Slaying Goliath", and "Cain and Abel" (1540-1549). Back in the church, on the first altar, "Descent of the Holy Spirit", another important painting by Titian executed in about 1555 for the Church of Santo Spirito. The second altar, dedicated to Saint Anthony of Padua, and the third, house two canvases by Pietro Liberi, "St. Anthony in Venice" and the "Annunciation". At the side of the church is the Patriarchal Seminary with a museum and gallery.

Basilica of the Salute, sacristy.
Titian, "St. Mark and Saints"

Basilica of the Salute

Basilica of the Salute. Dome

The Fondamenta delle Zattere, is thus called because it was here that rafts or lighters carrying wood were berthed. Saloni or Depositi del Sale (Salt warehouses) were reconstructed in the 19th century by A. Pigazzi.

The long Fondamenta (paved walkway running beside the water) delle Zattere runs along the length of the city's southern shore, from the Point of the Customs House down to San Basilio, where the port area begins. The Fondamenta faces on to the Canale della Giudecca, named after the island lying on the other side of it. Along the northern shore of the island the Venetian aristocracy constructed houses and villas with gardens and orchards and nurseries behind them.

A famous landmark on the island is the **Church of the Redentore**, built according to plans by Palladio between 1577 and 1592, and consecrated the year of its completion. Like the church of La Salute, this church, too, was erected after cessation of the plague of 1576. On the third Sunday of July each year the famous Redeemer's Feast is celebrated. Even today it touches the lives of Venetians. They come in vast crowds o the island, which is joined to the Zattere for the occasion by a pontoon-bridge. In the evening the Feast continues on the water: a large number of boats of all kinds gather in the Canal and the Venetians watch the splendid firework displays as they eat and drink.

Correr. Museum G. Heintz,
"Redentore Procession"

Continuing along the shore of the Zattere, further on is the **Church of St. Mary of the Rosary** or of the Gesuati. The Company of the Poor Gesuati, formed toward the end of the 14th century in Venice, built an oratory here between 1494 and 1524. The order was suppressed later, when the activities of the brothers went beyond the terms of reference deemed proper to their ministry, and the Dominicans took over. It was they who built the present church beside the previously-mentioned structures, starting in 1726 on plans by Giorgio Massari and finishing in 1736.

The church consists of a single nave with intercommunicating lateral chapels. On the ceiling between decora-

Santa Maria Dei Gesuati Church

tions and stuccoes, are three luminous frescoes (1737-1739) by G. Battista Tiepolo, the "*Institution of the Rosary*", the "*Apotheosis of St. Dominic*" and "*St. Dominic Blessing*". In the first chapel on the right there is a canvas, again by Tiepolo, painted about 1740. It represents the "*Virgin and St. Catherine of Siena and Two Other Saints*". In the second and third chapels are two paintings by Piazzetta. The first is much deteriorated, and represents the "*Likeness of St. Dominic*" (1743); the second shows "*Saints Vincent Ferrer and Hyacinthe and Louis Bertrand*" (1737). On the left wall, the "*Crucifixion*" by Tintoretto (1555-1560) in the first chapel, and "*Pius V and Saints*" by Sebastiano Ricci (1734) in the third, deserve study.

From the Church of the Gesuati, as we proceed along the Rio Terrà Marco Foscarini, we arrive at the Accademia with the Gothic church now housing the Academy of Fine Arts and the ex-monastery whose courtyard is still faced by the surviving wing of the Cloister erected by Palladio around 1552. The rest of the building was demolished and substituted by a double gallery by G. A. Selva around 1810, during conversion of rooms in the Picture Gallery. Adjacent is the School of St. Mary of Charity, one of the six large "schools" in the city. Its façade was erected by B. Maccaruzzi, probably according to designs by G. Massari.

The Accademia Galleries are now being rearranged. Some rooms are closed, and the placement of paintings may be modified.

Here we find the main entrance to the **Accademia Galleries**, containing a collection of highly-important paintings. By way of the large main staircase, dating back to the 17th century, we come to the Chapter Room, where we may admire the original ceiling, carved and gilded by Marco Cozzi in 1484. This room presents numerous altar-pieces and panels on gold grounds painted by Venetian masters between the 13th century

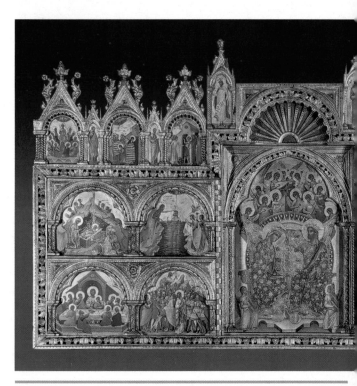

and the first half of the 15th. These paintings are in the Byzantine tradition, but steadily evolve toward Gothic forms influenced by Continental movements. Among the most important works are the Polyptych with episodes from the life of Christ, St. Francis and the Coronation of the Virgin, all in various compartments painted by Paolo Veneziano; a "*Madonna and Child Enthroned*", by the same painter, a "*Madonna and Child*" of the Veneto-Byzantine school in the 13th century. There is a large fourteenth-century Polyptych on two levels by Lorenzo Veneziano representing the "*Annunciation and Saints*" (1357); the

Polyptych "*St. James the Greater between Four Saints*" and the "*Coronation of the Virgin*", from the mid 15th century, were painted by Michele Giambono. We also find works by Michele di Matteo, Giovanni da Bologna, Jacobello Alberegno, Catarino, Antonio Vivarini, Nicolò di Pietro, Stefano and Jacopo Maranzone.

Room II, called the Hall of the Assumption (since Titian's masterpiece by that title was once exhibited here; now it is once again in the church of the Frari, in its original setting). In this room we find works by Giovanni Bellini, the "*Holy Family*" (1480-90) and the "*Mourning of Christ*". Works by Cima da Conegliano include the "*Incredulity of St. Thomas*", the "*Madonna of the Orange Tree*" (signed), and the "*Virgin and Child*" (1496-1499). Carpaccio painted the "*Presentation of Jesus in the Temple*", signing and dating it Marco Basaiti painted "*Jesus Praying in the Garden*".

Room III presents canvases by painters of the end of the 15th and the first half of the 16th centuries, including "*Saints Louis and Sinbald*" and "*Saints Sebastian and Basthdumén*" by Sebastiano dal Piombo a follower of Giorgione. There are also works by Giovanni Buonconsiglio, Cima da Conegliano and Benedetto Rusconi, called Diana.

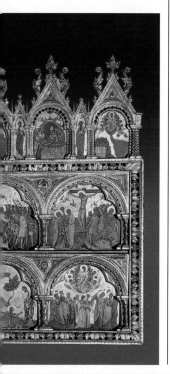

Paolo Veneziano, Polyptych.
Coronation of the Virgin

Sebastiano del Piombo, St Louis

Sebastiano del Piombo, San Sinibald

Room IV contains three precious paintings of the Italian 15th century: "Saint George" by Andrea Mantegna (1464), "St. Jerome" by Piero della Francesca (mid 15th century), and "Madonna and the Infant Jesus" by Cosmè Tura. Further paintings by Jacopo and Giovanni Bellini represent the "Madonna and Child". While Jacopo (Giovanni's father) still seems bound to the Gothic tradition, Giovanni, even in this painting of his youthful period, opens a new way of painting for future Venetian art. The Flemish painter, Hans Memling, is also present; his "Portrait of a Young Man" was once attributed to Antonello da Messina.

Room V is dedicated to works by Giovanni Bellini. Here the greatness and originality of the Venetian master shows up plainly, particularly in the "Madonna of the Little Trees" (1487) and the "Pietà". Other canvases are the "Madonna between Saints John the Baptist and Mary Magdalene". This room also contains one of the most famous paintings by Giorgione: the "Tempest" (1505-1507), which bears witness to an important stage in the process of innovation in taste and compositional conceptions in Venetian painting. The "Portrait of an Old Woman" by the same painter, expresses the nature of the human condition.

Room VI. We find works by Alessandro Bonvicino or Moretto, Paolo Caliari or Veronese "*Coronation of the Virgin*", Titian "*St John the Baptist*", Tintoretto "*Creation of the animals*" and Adam and Eve.

Room VII contains one of the most fascinating portraits of all time, Lorenzo Lotto's "*Young Man in his Study*" and works by Giovanni Busi, Moretto and Bernardino Licinio. "*Portrait of a Lady*".

Room VIII offers painters of the 16th century: numerous canvases by Bonifacio de' Pitati including "*St. Francis and St. Andrew*", "*St. Bernard and St. Sebastian*", and the "*Slaughter of the Innocents*"; and two paintings by J. Palma the Elder, the "*Assumption*" and the "*Virgin with Infant and Saints*". We also find here one of the most important painters from Brescia operating in Venice during the 16th century, Girolomo Romani called il Romanino, with his "*Deposition*".

Room IX is now closed.

Room X. Here we find the most important representatives of Venetian

Piero Della Francesca, St Jerome and the Portrait of the Donor

Paolo Veronese, "Feast in Levi's House"

painting in the second half of the 16th century: Tiziano Vecellio (Titian), Jacopo Robusti, known as Tintoretto, and Paolo Caliari, called Veronese. The canvases by Tintoretto belong to the cycle executed for the main hall of the School of Saint Mark, with episodes from the life of the Evangelist. The most famous of them is the "*Miracle of St Mark*". On the right-hand wall as we enter is the vast painting by Veronese, the "*Feast in Levi's House*".

Room XI presents numerous canvases by Veronese (1581); "*Madonna and Child*"; the "*Crucifixion*", the "*Assumption*" the "*Battle of Lepanto*" and the "*Allegory of Venice*". In the second half of the room we find a group of masters of the 17th and 18th centuries.

Room XII exhibits Venetian landscape painters of the 18th century, including G. Zais, M. Ricci, F. Zuccarelli.

Room XIII: in addition to a series of portraits by Tintoretto representing Procurators and Doge Alvise Mocenigo, we find portraits or religious subjects by J. and L. Bassano and "*Madonna and Child*" by Titian

Room XIV is devoted to seventeenth-century painters such as Domenico Fetti, Johann Liss and Bernardo Strozzi.

Giorgione, The Tempest. Below Giorgione, The Tempest (detail)

Room XV contains canvases by G. Battista Tiepolo "*Holy Family*" and "*St Cajetan*"; Antonio Pellegrini "*Sculpture and Painting*"; G. Battista Pittoni "*Adoration of the Magi*", the "*Rest in Egypt*". A small room follows, dedicated to Tiepolo, with four canvases depicting mythological subjects.

Room XVI Various works by G.B. Tiepolo and Sebastiano Ricci.

Room XVIA presents works by G. Battista Piazzetta, the last great Venetian ending the period of change initiated by Michelangelo and beginning a new path destined to be followed and widened by Tiepolo. The most admirable canvas is the famous "*Fortune Teller*", portraying the youthful and humorous likeness of a woman, smiling with subtle seductiveness. Other fine portraits are by Pietro and Alessandro Longhi.

Room XVII is divided into three sections. The first is devoted to vedutisti and landscape-painters, with Canaletto, Francesco Guardi, Michele Marieschi and Antonio Diziani. The

second includes figure-painters with sketches and drawings by Sebastiano Ricci, G. Battista Piazzetta, Jacopo Amigoni and G. Battista Pittoni; there is an early sketch by G. Battista Tiepolo, "*St. Dominic in Glory*". The third section shows Tiepolo's design for the fresco on the ceiling of the Church of the Scalzi (destroyed by bombardment during the First World War); Pietro Longhi, with a group of his characteristic genre paintings; and a group of pastels by Rosalba Carriera. Venetian eighteenth-century painting is represented here in all its diverse aspects and tendencies. Several sculptures by A. Canova are worth our attention.

Room XIX once more takes up the exhibition of works by fifteenth-century masters, continuing into the early years of the 16th century: Antonello da Saliba, Pietro da Messina, Vincenzo Catena, Marco Parziale.

Room XX presents an exhibition of teleri (Venetian term meaning a very large canvas in a cycle or series of historical or mythological works) which were once in the School of St.

Vittore Carpaccio, Story of St Ursula. Ursula meets Ereus and the Pilgrims Depart

John the Evangelist. They illustrate the "*Miracles of the Relic of the True Cross*" with its architecture, its people, its nobility and government, the City passes before our eyes, recreating unforgettable moments of its art, history and customs. The "*Miracle of the Relic Fallen into the Canal of San Lorenzo*" is by Gentile Bellini (1500), as is the "*Procession in Saint Mark's Square*" (1496); the cortege winds in all its magnificence from the Porta della Carta around the Square and is about to enter the Basilica, resplendent with its mosaics. Among other things, one may note the Procuratie Vecchie, which are Byzantine in style; the Orseolo Hospice backing on to the Campanile; and the Canons' houses.

The other large and equally famous painting is the "*Miraculous Healing of the Demoniac*", in which Vittore Carpaccio sets the scene at Rialto, with the Grand Canal and the old wooden bridge once crossing it. The painter succeeds admirably in recreating the busy life of that part of the city, concerned with commerce and traffic, with its continuous crisscrossing of small boats and gondolas, and people grouped on the sides of the canal.; an imaginary loggia sits on the left, in the shelter of the Palace of the Patriarch of Grado. The other canvases are by Giovanni Mansueti (the "*Miracle at San Lio*" and the, in which we see the interior of a Venetian house of the time); by Lazzaro Bastiani (the "*Offering of the*

Gentile Bellini, Procession of the Cross in San Mark's Square (det.)

Vittore Carpaccio, Story of St Ursula. The English Ambassadors return home

Relic in the Church of St John the Evangelist"); and by Benedetto Diana (the *"Child Saved by the Relic"*)

Room XXI. Towards the end of the 15th century Vittore Carpaccio was engaged in painting the famous *teleri* for the School of St. Ursula, which was founded in 1306, located near the Church of Saints John and Paul. The painter illustrated significant episodes from the legendary life of the Saint, taken from a thirteenth-century Chronicle written by Jacopo da Varagine. The pleasantly imaginative, even fantastic, narrative gifts of Carpaccio

are fully exploited here: *"Ambassadors of the English King Present their Credentials to the King of Britany and Ask for the Hand of Princess Ursula in Marriage for the Son of the English King"*, *"The King of Brittany Consigns his Reply to the Ambassadors"*, the *"Ambassadors Return to England"*, the *"Wedding"*, the *"Two Betrothed Are Received by Pope Cyriac"*, the *"Dream of Ursula"*, the *"Arrival at Cologne Besieged by the Huns"*, the *"Martyrdom of the Christians and with them Ursula, at Cologne"*, the *"Apotheosis of Saint Ursula"*. Although portraying a foreign city and foreign setting, the scenes are worked out in Venetian terms and

Titian. The Presentation
of the Viergin in the Temple

Vittore Carpaccio.
Miraculous Healing of the Demoniac

minutely detailed; an example is the interior of Ursula's room. The ceremonials are inspired by the protocol of Venetian diplomacy, and the personages portrayed are actual members of the School of Saint Ursula in Venice.

Room XXII. The exposition of the paintings is now to be re-ordered.

Room XXIV was in old times the Albergo della Scuola, with its rich ceiling carved in 1496. It contains two remarkable works: the "Presentation of the Virgin at the Temple" by Titian (1538), and the large triptych, the "Virgin and Child Enthroned between the Doctors of the Church" by Antonio Vivarini and Giovanni d'Alemagna: truly expressive.

Gentile Bellini. Miracle of the Relic Fallen into the Canal of San Lorenzo (detail)

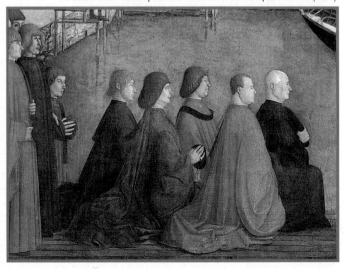

Church of San Vidal

Leaving the Accademia and crossing the Grand Canal by way of the wooden bridge first constructed by the Austrians in 1854, then reconstructed by Miozzi in 1932, you come into Campo Santo Stefano, one of the largest and most striking open spaces in Venice.

Here in the old days rich festivals were held with the participation of large numbers of people, and the last bullfight in Venice was held here in 1802.

The **Church of San Vidal** stands at the opening of the square. It was founded in the 11th century. The present construction is of the 16th century, after plans by Gaspari, while the façade was erected by A. Tirali at the beginning of the 18th century.

Three important paintings are to be found in the interior: *"San Vitale on Horseback with Saints"* by Vittore Carpaccio, the *"Immaculate Conception"* by Sebastiano Ricci, and the *"Archangel Raphael and Saints"* by G. B. Piazzetta (1730 circa).

On the right is the Pisani Palace, now the seat of the Music Conservatory, named after the famous eighteenth-century composer Benedetto Marcello.

Construction of the building was

started at the beginning of the 17th century after plans by Bartolomeo Monopola and was completed by Frigimelica, who raised the elevation a floor higher.

At the far side of the Campo, the side of the **Church of Santo Stefano** closes the whole complex. The present building goes back to the 14th century (it was finished in 1374), and is of the conventual type, with three naves, a presbytery and a crypt below. The façade was enhanced in the early 15th century with a fine doorway by Bartolomeo Bon. The decorated ceiling, with its wooden structure in the shape of a ship's keel, is of the same period. The wooden choir, was demolished, and the stalls reassembled behind the main altar.

The **Theatre** has been an important social institution and one of the major attractions in Venice. (Nearly all the numerous other theatres which once existed have been demolished.).

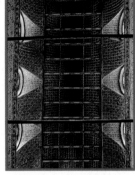

Church of Santo Stefano. The Ceiling

Campo and Church of Santo Stefano

La Fenice was opened as late as 1792, a few years before the fall of the Republic, which had entrusted its construction to Antonio Selva. It was almost completely destroyed by fire in 1836 (as it would be in 1997), but was soon reconstructed by the Meduna brothers, who made every attempt possible to preserve the original eighteenth-century taste. The rest of the building consists of other halls in neo-classical style.

After the bridge, we encounter the **Church of San Moisé**, which has a very early origin indeed, perhaps dating back to the 18th century. It was reconstructed originally in the 13th century, but what remains of this first structure is only the fine campanile. Work on the present building began in 1632. In 1668 Alessandro Tremignon started the façade. Continuing in the same direction you soon reach Saint Mark's Square.

If you wish to prolong your route somewhat between Campo Santo Stefano and Piazza San Marco, you may include the **Church of Santa Maria del Giglio** by following a series of calli and squares till you arrive through Calle delle Ostreghe at the campo where this church stands. Founded in the 9th century, the church was later reconstructed. It has a single nave. The rich façade was completed by Giuseppe Sardi between 1678 and 1683.

Contarini Dal Bovolo Palace is in calle Della Vida n. 4299. (Arch. G. Candi, circa 1499). It gains renown from the spiral exterior staircase.

Palazzo Contarini Dal Bovolo

La Fenice Theatre

ITINERARY

SS. GIOVANNI AND PAOLO

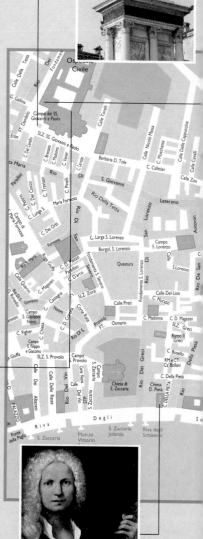

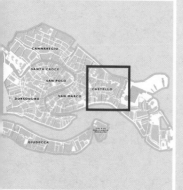

Basilica of SS. Giovanni and Paolo.
Monument to the doge Zeno

Portrait of
Antonio Vivaldi

Campo SS. Giovanni and Paolo.
Andrea Verrocchio, Equestrian Statue
to Bartolomeo Colleoni

Rio della Misericordia.
School of St Mark. Façade

Arsenal, Portal. Scupltures

From Piazza San Marco, Ponte della Paglia and Riva degli Schiavoni. In front of the Equestrian Monument to Victor Emanuel II is the covered passageway through which you reach **Campo San Zaccaria**, where the church of that name stands with a monastery attached. This was one of the most important religious complexes of the city.

It was founded by Doge Giustiniano Partecipazio (827-829). In the 13th century and the first half of the 14th, the building further developed. From this period there remain the bell-tower and the apse area, which is called the Chapel of San Tarasio. In Gothic style, it conserves the remains of antique pavements in marble mosaic.

The left nave of this building was incorporated in the new one, in the church built in the 15th century.

From these beginnings rose the great new church which we see today, and which Antonio Gambello started to construct from the apse area toward the façade in 1458. In 1480 Mauro Coducci continued the work of the of the first architect, who had worked in Gothic forms, and completed the building with the remaining naves and the façade.

Inside the church are three paintings by J. Palma the Younger, *"Madonna and Child Entroned"*, *"St Zacharias in Glory"*, and *"David and Goliath"*; an altarpiece by Giovanni Bellini, the *"Virgin and Child Enthroned"*, a work

A. Canal. Visit of the doge to San Zaccaria

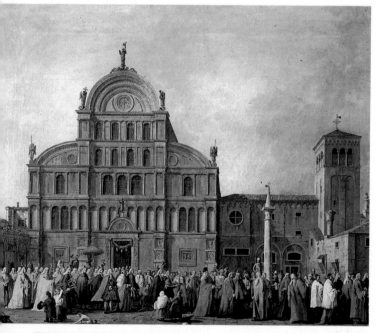

signed and dated 1505. In the Chapel of San Tarasio, a large polyptych, *"Santa Sabina"*, which dates back to 1443 and is the work of Giovanni and Antonio da Murano.

San Zaccaria with Cloisters. Aerial View

Church of the Pietà. Interior

The **Church of the Pietà** and the Hospice. The church, dating from the 15th century, was reconstructed by Giorgio Massari between 1745 and 1760. The interior has one nave and an oval floor plan, with frescoes by Tiepolo: on the ceiling of the entrance, *"Strength and Peace"*, on the central ceiling, the *"Triumph of Faith"*, and in the presbytery, the *"Cardinal Virtues"*, work carried out in 1754 and 1755. There is also an altarpiece, the *"Visitation"*, by G. B. Piazzetta, left unfinished because of the master's death.

The Hospice of the Pietà, founded in 1346, and at one time known as the Foundling hospital, in time came to serve the specialised purpose of providing for the maintenance and musical education of young female orphans. Celebrated in this institute and others of the city such as San Lazzaro dei Mendicanti, were the public concerts held in the church by these young artists on stands specially built high up along the walls, and linked directly to the dormitories. The main body of the church was transformed into a concert hall, and was often crowded with an enthusiastic public of Venetians and foreigners. The Hospice has remained famous ever since it had as its choirmster -for forty years! - the Venetian composer Antonio Vivaldi, who was known as the red priest, on account of his red hair.

The **Arsenal** covers a vast inland harbour surrounded by high walls, in which from ancient times on, ships of the Republic's fleet were constructed and repaired.

Here, all the various activities connected with navigation were carried out; so there were rope factories, and workshops producing sail-cloth, sails and all sorts of other naval equipment and supplies. Tradition has it that the Arsenal was founded in 1104, and that from then on it continued to expand with ever larger basins and larger workshops. In 1325 the Casa del Canevo was constructed, where ropes and rigging were made. This building was reconstructed by Antonio da Ponte in 1570; then it measured more than 300 metres in length and was subdivided into three corridors. The Main Entrance Gate, planned by Antonio Gambello, was perhaps one of the first Renaissance structures in Venetian architecture, dating back to 1460. Around 1547 the Bucentaur shipyard was erected to house the great ceremonial ship several levels

Arsenal. The Water Entrance

Arsenal Portal

high, and with two hundred oars, the whole decorated in gold with wooden inlay work and mythological and symbolic sculpted figures. It had a high poop, on which the Doge and the Signoria took their places during the most important ceremonies each year. The first and foremost was the Wedding of the Sea, which took place annually.

Upon leaving the Arsenal, and following a series of squares and lanes, you reach **San Giovanni in Bragora**, a quiet, sunny square with the Gothic church founded in the 9th century and rebuilt about 1475 with elements in the façade indicating the then new Renaissance taste.

School of San Giorgio degli Schiavoni. On the Fondamenta dei Furlani, we encounter a building dating back to the early 16th century. The interior is still visited because it contains the precious cycle of paintings by Vittore Carpaccio, dating from 1502-1509, representing stories of three Dalmatian saints: *"Episodes from the Life of St. George"*, including *"St George Killing the Dragon"*, the *"Triumph of St George"* and the Saint *"Baptising the King and Queen of Libya"* (signed and dated 1508); *"Episodes from the Life of St. Trifon of Bithynia"* and *"Life of St. Jerome"*, Bishop of Split, including the *"Lion Tamed"*, *"Saint Augustine in his Study"* and the *"Funeral of St Jerome"*, signed and dated 1502.

Church of San Giovanni in Bragora

V. Carpaccio. Saint Augustine in his Study

In Campo **San Francesco Della Vigna** we find the church of that name, and the monastery. The first building, of the 12th century, was reconstructed in the Gothic period between the 14th and 15th centuries. From this period we find three cloisters -two complete ones, and one partly demolished on two sides facing the lagoon, during Napoleon's time. The Church was rebuilt by Sansovino between 1534 and 1568, the façade completed by Palladio between 1568 and 1572. The interior has one nave only, with deep recessed chapels. On the altar of the Chapel of the Conception is the *"Virgin and Child between Saints"* by Giovanni Bellini, signed and dated 1507. In the sacristy we can admire the *"Holy Family"* by P. Veronese.

Campo SS. Giovanni and Paolo. We now find ourselves in one of the most striking urban layouts of the city, embracing the monumental church called the School of Saint Mark, now entrance-hall to the Civil Hospital of Venice; and the Equestrian Monument to Bartolomeo Colleoni, the most famous soldier of fortune in the service of the Republic. The equestrian statue was erected in 1488 after the model made by Andrea Verrocchio; Alessandro Leopardi designed the pedestal.

The side of the Campo facing the Church borders on the Canale dei Mendicanti, named after the Hospice that rises on the Fondamenta.

The Church of Saints John and Paul is built on an area given by the Republic to the Dominican Order, which started

Campo SS. Giovanni and Paolo. The School, the Basilica and the Monument

the construction in the 13th century. Building went on for some two centuries; as with Santa Maria dei Frari, it began in the apse area, which was completed together with the transept towards 1368. Work was then continued towards the façade and finished in 1430, the year of the church's consecration. Following a bequest in 1458, construction began on the new façade, according to designs by Antonio Gambello.

The interior with three naves, on the plan of an Egyptian cross with five absidal chapels, gives the same impression of grandeur that we find in Santa Maria dei Frari, augmented in this case by the strong illumination due to the southward exposure of the apses. The church followed immediately after San Marco in importance: the Doges are buried here.

Above the entrance portal we see monuments to Doge Alvise Mocenigo (died 1577) and his wife, by the architect Gerolamo Grapiglia, with sculptures by A. Vittoria; and to Doge Pietro Mocenigo (died 1476) by Pietro Lombardo, one of the most significant Renaissance works. On the second altar to the right in a carved and gilded frame we find the precious polyptych attributed to Giovanni Bellini, executed around 1465.

The Chapel of St. Dominic is a sumptuous architectural complex, build according to designs by Andrea Tirali at the beginning of the 18th century. On the ceiling vault, carved and richly gilded, is the very fine painting by G. Battista Piazzetta (1727), the *"Glorification of St Dominic"*. In the transept is *"Christ Carrying the Cross"* by Alvise Vivarini. On the altar which follows is Lorenzo Lotto's *"Saint Anthony Giving Alms"*, dated 1542. At the end of the transept, we see a large window in flamboyant Gothic style, with fifteenth-century glass which can be admired from the Campo outside as well. It is of Murano craftsmanship. Its stained glass depict figures of Saints, based on cartoons by B. Vivarini.

In the presbytery we encounter various

Monument to Colleoni

monuments. That dedicated to Doge Andrea Vendramin is one of the most significant Renaissance works. It is attributed to the Lombardos, both

because of the proportions of the group as a whole and the expressive perfection of the statues.

Coming out into the left transept again, you can see an equestrian statue of gilded wood, attributed to Lorenzo Bregno. Next are the surviving pieces of a polyptych by Bartolomeo Vivarini, signed and dated 1473. Also, a large eighteenth-century organ by Gaetano Calido.

Basilica of SS. Giovanni and Paolo. Aerial View

School of Saint Mark

Going along the left nave we find a monument to Doge Pasquale Malipiero (died 1462), a Renaissance work by Pietro Lombardo; an altar dedicated to the daughter of Mastino Della Scala, by Guglielmo Grigi from Bergamo, dating from about 1525; and an altar painting showing "*Magdalene before the Cross*", by Pietro Liberi.

To the side of the church we find

Campo Santa Maria Formosa.

the **School of Saint Mark**, instituted in 1260 with the name "Dei Battuti". The original premises were destroyed in 1485, and the present edifice was begun in 1487, according to designs by Pietro Lombardo in collaboration with his sons Tullio and Antonio, with Antonio Buora. Three years after, in 1490, Lombardo was dismissed by the commissioning authority, and the work entrusted to Mauro Coducci, who completed the façade with the typical curvilinear crown and built the grand staircase.

The **Church of Santa Maria Formosa** seems to have been founded in the 8th century. Ancient legends relate that the Virgin, resembling a beautiful matron, appeared to St. Magnus, Bishop, in a dream. The building was reconstructed many times, lastly by Mauro Coducci, starting in 1491.

However, construction work was interrupted, and not until 1542 was the façade toward the canal erected. The lateral one, toward the Campo, was completed as late as 1604. The church is unique in form, as much for the resolution of its lateral façade problems as for the belfry and pinnacle of the campanile, which was executed from designs by the priest Francesco Zuccoli between 1611 and 1688. The keystone of the arch at the entrance-door to the Campanile is an amusing grotesque mask.

The interior of the church is a Latin cross adapted to the pre-existing Greek cross pattern. It has three naves, and a transept with cross vaults. The organ on the wall of the front entrance was made in 1542. Above the altar in the Chapel of the Conception, the first in the right nave, there is a triptych by Bartolomeo Vivarini, signed and dated 1473, with *"Our Lady of Mercy and Other Episodes from the Life of the Virgin"*.

Continuing along the right nave, we see the *"Pietà"* by J. Palma the Younger and the *"Last Supper"* by J. Bassano. Then comes the Chapel of the School of the Bombardieri, the makers of bombards, an early form of cannon. The celebrated painting by J. Palma the Elder (1480-1510) represents *"Santa Barbara"*, protectress of the School.

Walking round the outside of the apse, you come to the Campiello Querini-Stampalia, named after the family who built the palace overlooking the canal, at the beginning of the 16th century.

This building is now the seat of the Querini-Stampalia Library. The name "Stampalia" comes from the island where certain members of the family were exiled after taking part in the Baja-

monte Tiepolo conspiracy in 1310. There is also a Picture Gallery here which houses a large number of interesting paintings, among which stand out sixty-nine works by Gabriele Bella done in the mid 18th century.

Santa Maria Formosa, bell-tower

Campiello Querini Stampalia

Campo of
Ghetto Nuovo

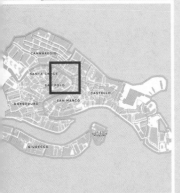

Pesaro Palace

Rialto Bridge
and the Regata

Ca' D'Oro

Imaginary Portrait
of Marco Polo

Campo San Batolomeo.
Monument to Carlo Goldoni

From the very origins of the city, whose religious and political centre was Saint Mark's Square, Rialto became the economic centre. In this area, each in its special zone, were the fish market, the fruit and vegetable market, the goldsmiths' shops, cloth shops and various markets dealing in spices and raw materials in general. Rialto's Church of San Giovanni Elemosinario was born and grew up amidst the markets. It has been rebuilt many times; the last reconstruction, made according to plans by Scarpagnino, was in the period between 1527 and 1539. The Church of San Giacomo di Rialto also dates back to this period. Situated in the Campo of the same name, it maintains in the interior the original twelfth-century structure. It was partially reconstructed later, when the portico outside the façade was added. In the early days many patricians - or at any rate, rich families - lived in the market area. Later, as it became the most popu-

Rialto, Fish Market

lar area, they moved to other parts of the city, in the direction of San Polo and along the Grand Canal. As commerce grew, the residential area extended even into the adjacent zone of San Matteo.

The Rialto Market and the façade of the Church of S. Giacometto

Rialto, Fish Market

Modern Art Gallery, Ca' Pesaro. On exhibit here are works by Italian and foreign artists of the 19th and 20th centuries, with emphasis on Venetian art.

Amongst the landscape-painters of the second half of the 19th century are Giacomo Favretto and Guglielmo Ciardi. Those of the early 20th century include Luigi Nono, Pietro Fragiacomo, Alessandro Milesi, and then the pointillists or divisionisti, Gaetano Previati and Giovanni Segantini. Sculptures include works by Alberto Viani, Luigi Borro, Arturo Martini and Medardo Rosso. The latter is present here with a group of works of exceptional interest. Foreign artists included are Emile Claus, Frank Brongwyn, Wilhelm Leibl, and Max Liebermann. The Burano group includes Tullio Garbari, Ugo Valeri, Umberto Moggioli; more modern artists include Boccioni, Martini, Pio Semeghini, Felice Casorati, and Felice Carena. On the second floor are more works by artists already named above, plus Federigo Zandomeneghi and, among the Tuscan Macchiaioli, Telemaco Signorini and Giovanni Fattori.

On the top floor is the **Oriental Art Museum.**

Pesaro Palace.
Medardo Rosso,
"Head of a Youth"

155

Ca' D'Oro. The fine collection inside was presented to the State by Giorgio Franchetti.

You reach the first floor by the open-air staircase (once protected by a wooden covering); it contains works by Matteo Raverti. In the sala portego, the central hall, one has a splendid view of the Grand Canal from the balcony.

He we find busts of Procurators by Vittoria near a marble lunette by J. Sansovino. In the first room to the left are a two paintings by Vittore Carpaccio, the *"Annunciation"* and the *"Dormition of the Virgin"*, which at one time belonged to the cycle of paintings in the School of the Albanesi.

Transferred from another site, the coffered ceiling was adapted to this room housing Titian's *"Venus"*, by some

Ca' D'Oro, Franchetti Gallery.
V. Gambello, *"Battle between Satyrs and Giants"*

deemed to be the most important painting of the entire collection. Going out on the side of the rear courtyard we find *"St Sebastian"* by Andrea Mantegna. In the transverse wing, where the 16th-century wooden ceiling has been adapted, is the *"Queen of Sheba and Solomon"* by Francesco Da Ponte, known as Bassano. In the main hall is the *"Portrait of a Knight"* by Anthony Van Dyck.

If you wish to see the populous quarter of Cannaregio, walk from the Cà d'Oro along the Strada Nuova **Cannaregio**. This sestiere is picturesque and unusual in layout, since it consists of long, narrow islands separated by parallel canals. The majority of these islands, especially those near the edge of the lagoon, were created over the centuries by building up the shoals. The most important and significant monuments include the Church and New School of the Misericordia (built by Sansovino but with an unfinished façade); the Church

Ca' D'Oro, Franchetti Gallery.
Andrea Mantegna, *"Saint Sebastian"*

Bridges and Houses in Ghetto Nuovissimo

of the Madonna dell'Orto (another notable example of fifteenth-century Gothic architecture), recently and magnificently restored; the Church of Sant'Alvise, the

Ghetto (where Jews were required to live under the Republic), and the Schools or synagogues there, representing the various rites according to the origins of different groups. Among these Schools, the 17th-cent. temple by Longhena is noteworthy.

The **Church of Santa Maria Dei Gesuiti** was built according to plans by Domenico Rossi, between 1714 and 1729; the façade is attributed to G. B. Fattoretto. This area was acquired by the Jesuits from the original owners, the ancient Order of the Hospitalers (known as the Crociferi). The former School of the Crociferi is opposite the church and was founded by Doge Zeno in the second half of the 13th century.

The Church of the Jesuits follows the Latin cross in plan and the lateral chapels are sumptuously decorated with stuccoes, marbles and statues.

Numerous paintings by Jacopo Palma the Younger grace the altar, and on the left is the famous *"Martyrdom of Saint Lawrence"* (1558) by Titian. This work is a nocturnal scene illuminated by torches and blazing coals.

Campo of the Ghetto

Santa Maria Dei Miracoli. This small Renaissance edifice was erected by Pietro Lombardo between 1481 and 1489, and is one of the most representative expressions of the new artistic language of the Renaissance. Unlike many others in Venice, this church has remained unaltered. Limited by existing buildings, the church occupies a long, narrow site abutting the Rio dei Miracoli. Both the exterior and interior walls are completely covered with slabs of polychrome marble, decorated with inlaid work in designs and strips creating architectural bays. The presbytery is raised

Church of the Miracoli

Campiello of Milion

above the crypt in the single nave. Behind the church is the Malibran Theatre, named after the celebrated opera singer who performed there in 1834. It was first opened by Giovanni Grimani in 1678 under the name of Saint John Chrysostom Theatre. Regrettably this theatre has been restored a number of times; it was completely restructured in 1920, and is now a cinema. Alongside the theatre is the Campiello del Milion, whose buildings bear traces of tenth- to eleventh-century Byzantine style. The small square's name derives from the Polo family, who owned several houses here. Their famous son, Marco, journeyed as far east as the Court of the Grand Mogul, where he stayed from 1271 to 1275. Marco was taken prisoner by the Genoese during the famous battle of the Curzolari in 1298. During his imprisonment in Genua he dictated the contents of his famous book, Milione, a chronicle of his journeys.

On your right is the German Merchants' Warehouse, "Fondaco dei Tedeschi", and a little further on, Campo San Bartolomeo, on the opposite side of the Rialto Bridge, from where you began your itinerary. This Campo is a famous gathering place for much of the city's populace, lying at the intersection of three sestieri: San Marco, Cannaregio and San Polo. In the centre stands the monument to Carlo Goldoni, the famous eighteenth-century Venetian playwright.

From here continue to **Campo San Salvador** with its church of the same name, constructed between 1507 and 1534 after plans by Antonio Spavento, who was later substituted by the Lom-

Campo San Bartolomio

Church of Saint Salvador. Interior

bardos and by Sansovino. The façade was added by G. Sardi in 1663.

The plan of this church consists of three naves together with three central cupolas. To gain extra light in the interior, Scamozzi opened the three lanterns (1574). Sansovino also worked on the interior. He designed the monument to Doge Francesco Venier (died 1556) as well as the 3rd altar on the right, with its altarpiece, Titian's *"Annunciation"*.

The **Mercerie**. Flanked entirely by shops, it originates at Campo San Salvador to form the most important artery of the city. From the earliest times it has

Rangone, a physician from Ravenna, and his statue may be seen above the main portal.

Continue in the same direction and pass under the Clock Tower into Saint Mark's Square.

Church of San Zulian (det.)

Monument to Carlo Goldoni

connected the political and religious centre of Saint Mark's with the commercial centre of Rialto. Although Gothic traces remain at some points, almost all the shop fronts have been altered from the 16th century on through to the present day.

After crossing the Ponte dei Baretteri ("cap makers") you reach Campo San Zulian. The **Church of San Zulian** is of ancient foundation, and has required periodic restructuring. It was rebuilt towards the middle of the 16th century by the ageing J. Sansovino, with the collaboration of Alessandro Vittoria. The building was commissioned by Tommaso

⑥ ITINERARY

SAN ROCCO

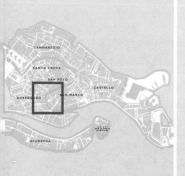

Saint Roch School.
Jacopo Tintoretto, Flight into Egypt

Cà Rezzonico.
Museum of 18th-century Venetian Art

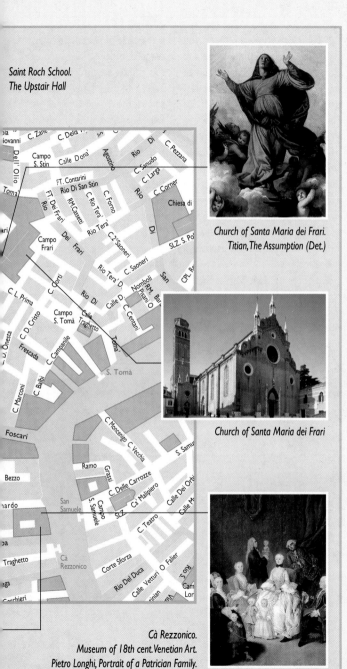

Saint Roch School.
The Upstair Hall

Church of Santa Maria dei Frari.
Titian, The Assumption (Det.)

Church of Santa Maria dei Frari

Cà Rezzonico.
Museum of 18th cent. Venetian Art.
Pietro Longhi, Portrait of a Patrician Family.

This 6th itinerary takes you mostly through the sestiere of Dorsoduro, with two brief detours at the beginning and end into the sestiere of Santa Croce and that of San Polo.

Straight ahead is the small **Church of San Nicolò Dei Mendicoli**, which is said to have been founded in the 7th century. During the second half of the 12th century it was completely rebuilt and the bell tower was added. During the 14th century the roof was replaced and the capitals of the nave changed.

Church of San Sebastiano. Nearby is the Church of Saint Sebastian built on a single nave by Antonio Abbondi (Scarpagnino) between 1505 and 1548. The chief point of interest

is the cycle of paintings by Paolo Veronese. In order to follow the work of this painter in chronological order, begin with the sacristy, where you can admire the *"Virgin Crowned, with the Evangelists"* (1555) on the ceiling. The paintings on the walls are the work of the school of Bonifacio Pitati. Back in the nave you may admire the three central panels on the ceiling (1556) by Veronese, *"Stories of Queen Esther"*. After completing these he frescoed the dome of the presbytery with the *"Assumption of the Virgin amid the Glory of Angels and the Doctors of the Church"*. These frescoes no longer exist. Meanwhile Veronese prepared the cartoons for the wall frescoes, completed later with the aid of his brother Benedetto and other follow-

Church of San Nicolò Dei Mendicoli

Church of San Sebastiano. P. Veronese, The Triumph of Mordechai

ers. The upper frieze displays architectural motifs with twisted spiral columns among which a series of Prophets and Sybils alternate. The *"Annunciation"* is on the arch above the high altar, and the partly effaced *"Apostles"* appears on the spandrels of the six lateral chapels. Veronese decorated the main altarpiece in 1559 with the *"Virgin and Child in Glory with Saints Sebastian, Peter, Catherine and Francis"*. During the same period he prepared the designs for the organ. On the exterior of the shutters he depicted the *"Presentation of Jesus in the Temple"* and on the interior, the *"Pool of Bethesda"*.

The *"Nativity"*, together with allegorical figures and saints, is painted on the parapet. In 1565 he began the decoration of the main chapel with *"Episodes from the Life of Saint Sebastian"*. The last painting was completed in 1570 for the refectory of the friars, and represented *"Supper in the Pharisee's House"*, now in the Brera Gallery in Milan. The great master is buried here.

Cross the bridge over the Rio San Basilio and follow along the Fondamenta San Sebastiano.

From the corner beyond the Rio you can see Ca' Ariani, built in the 2nd half of the 14th century. Over the arches of the second storey a very rich and delicate tracery appears, prototype of many later Venetian palaces. At number 2597 Antonio Gaspari built the Zenobio Palace between the years 1690 and 1700. The interior, and especially the ball-room, are decorated with eighteenth-century stuccoes and frescoes.

Campo and Church of the Carmini. The Campo affords a view of the Church of the Carmini, founded in the 12th century (evidence of the founding date remains on the side door). The

Ariani Palace

Church and Campo of the Carmini

church was rebuilt in 1286 and reconsecrated in 1348. Built on a basilica plan with three naves, its tall columns bear fourteenth-century capitals. The Gothic structure of the church was somewhat modified at the beginning of the 16th century, both in the apse area and on the façade, which features the familiar curvilinear crown. Above the second altar on the right wall is an important reredos by Cima da Conegliano (1509 circa) representing the *"Nativity with Saints Helena and Catherine, the Guardian Angel and Tobias".*

The dome is decorated with frescoes by Sebastiano Ricci (1708). In the last bay of the central nave are the two projecting singing galleries for the organ and singers. Both date from the 16th century, but the one on the right was partly renovated during the 19th century. The pictorial decoration is by Andrea Schiavone.

School of the Carmini. Next to the church is the School of the Carmelites built during the second half of the 17th century and completed with the two façades between 1668 and 1670. During the 18th century the interiors were decorated by Tiepolo in 1744. The grand stairway is surmounted by vaults richly decorated with stuccoes and frescoes. Magnificent canvases by Tiepolo fill the nine compartments of the upper hall ceiling. In the centre, note the *"Virgin in Glory Offers the Scapular to the Blessed Simon Stock"* (English Carmelite friar who died at Aylesford, Kent, in 1265). Virtues and angels appear on the sides. Near the doorway leading from the Hall of the Archives to the Meeting Room is the excellent painting by G. Battista Piazzetta, *"Judith and Holofernes".*

The Rezzonico Palace overlooks the Grand Canal and is now the **Museum of 18th-Century Venetian Art** Construction of the palace was initiated by B. Longhena for the Bon family in 1667. When the architect died in 1682 the building had reached the first floor. In 1750, work recommenced under the Rezzonico family, who were the new owners. Giorgio Massari finished the building for them in 1753, adhering to Longhena's original project. Massari modified the rear of the building with a courtyard, monumental stairway and grandiose ballroom. The magnificent ceiling fresco was painted by G. Battista Crosato in collaboration with the perspective painter Pietro Visconti. The Hall of the Wedding Allegory is named after the ceiling fresco executed by G. Battista Tiepolo for the wedding of Lodovico Rezzonico and Faustina Savorgnan. All the furniture is original eighteenth-century Venetian.

The Pastel Room is named after the series of pastel portraits and miniatures executed by Rosalba Carriera. A self-portrait of the artist is also displayed here. In 1578, G. Battista Tiepolo frescoed the ceiling of the Throne Room with a luminous composition representing the *"Allegory of Merit"* among figures of angels and Virtues.

Go up to the second floor to enter the Portego Room, which has the same dimensions as the one on the floor below; eighteenth-century paintings are exhibited. A Venetian bedroom

Francesco Guardi. The Nun's Parlour

has been reconstructed in the Alcove Bedroom, complete with two small side-rooms made of lacquered and painted wood.

In the Longhi Room the ceiling is decorated with one of Gianbattista Tiepolo's most important early works, the *"Triumph of Zephyrus and Flora"*. Thirty-four paintings by Pietro Longhi adorn the walls.

A whole gallery of customs, costumes and habits peculiar to Venetian private life is presented with gentle satire and goodnatured humour. A cross-section of the populace is depicted in their most characteristic poses and surroundings, in *"Morning Chocolate"*, *"Lady's Toilet"*, *"Polenta"*, *"Painter's Studio"*, *"Horse Ride"*, *"Visit to*

Pietro Longhi. The Family Concert

the Convent", *"Family Concert"*, *"Bauta"*, *"Furlana"*, *"Spice Vendor*.

The Ridotto Room contains two celebrated canvases by Guardi, the *"Ridotto"* and *"Convent Parlour"*. Wealthy Venetian society was accustomed to meet in the famous rooms of the "Ridotto" or gambling house near San Moisè or in the Nun's Parlour at San Zaccaria, where worldliness and religiosity met in an atmosphere not lacking in its particular kind of licentiousness.

The next room contains a precious spinet, carved and decorated with country and hunting scenes. A series of smaller rooms has been used to house reconstructions of interiors from the Tiepolo Villa of Zianigo; the frescoes by Giandomenico were removed and transferred here. This artist, here liberated from his father's influence, freely interprets the frivolity of the Venetian world. He emphasises the gay and

169

carefree character of this society, which inspired him amid the countryside of the Veneto. The *"New World"* (1791) is a gay popular scene depicting a charlatan impressing a crowd of country folk on a Sunday feast day with the novelties and wonders of the "New World", in contrast to the society of the time. The elderly gentleman and the young man are said to be images of the painter himself, and his father. The *"Minuet in the Villa"* depicts a scene of countryside holiday-making by Venetian nobility. *"Promenade"* shows a lady out walking with two beaux.

The figure of the *"Clown"* dominates another room. Masked and clothed in white, he conceals his symbolism under the guise of a buffoon, in the "

G. Domenico Tiepolo. The Clowns

Pietro Longhi. The Toilet

Cà Rezzonico. Dancing Hall

Saltimbanco's House", *"Clowns at Rest"* and the " *Clown in Love"*.

A veiled melancholy shrouds the last of these frescoes in contrast to the ceiling fresco, where the clowns amuse themselves on a swing. A fine grey hound is depicted above the chimney piece. The Chapel was decorated with frescoes by Giandomenico in 1749

Cà Rezzonico. Alcove Bedroom

for the Rezzonico family, when he was twenty-two years old. Finally you reach the Centaur Room and the Satyr Room, so named because of the mythological scenes decorating them.

Proceed to the 3rd floor, containing a collection of china, porcelain, chinoiserie, ceramics, costumes, drawings, cartoons, minor paintings and so on. Two reconstructions are of exceptional interest. First, the eighteenth-century pharmacy, complete with all its furnishings -- jars for spices and herbs, glasses, a laboratory and burner, a still, retorts, phials and other apparatus. And then the Puppet Theatre whose performances were held in public theatres, noble houses and public squares.

Return to Campo San Barnaba and cross the Ponte dei Pugni, named in honour of the traditional fights that occurred there between the two hostile factions of the city, the Castellani (inhabitants of San Pietro di Castello) and the Nicolotti (from San Nicolò dei Mendicoli). The original bridge had no parapets, and the boxers ("fists") did their best to push their rivals over the side into the canal.

Proceed along the Rio Terà dei Pugni to Campo Santa Margherita, one of the oldest centres of the city.

Pietro Longhi. Portrait of a Patrician Family

Saint Roch School (Scuola Di San Rocco). Although begun in 1515, building went on for over fifty years. Bartolomeo Bon supervised the work up to the first floor, and Scarpagnino and Giangiacomo dei Grigi finished the structure. The twin-lighted windows on the ground floor are clearly inspired by Coducci. Scarpagnino arranged for the large jutting columns to be added on to the preceding design.

Portrait of J. Tintoretto

Between 1564 and 1588, Tintoretto painted one of his most important

Saint Roch School. Façade

cycles for this school. Having reached maturity by that time, he succeeded in expressing his original artistic concepts. He used strong lighting to bring out the dynamic qualities inherent in his large compositions, where individual figures are placed in relationships that depend on the use of daring and disconcerting perspective.

In the ground floor hall, eight large canvases along the walls narrate scenes from the New Testament including the *"Flight into Egypt"*. The first floor is reached by means of the monumental stairway whose vault was frescoed by Gerolamo Pellegrini. In the main hall are twenty-three canvases by Tintoretto, all commissioned by the School. He finished the ceiling pieces by 1578 and the mural by 1581. Framed by rich decoration, the ceiling canvases illustrate *"Episodes from the Old Testament"* while those on the wall narrate episodes from the *"New Testament"*. The large ceiling paintings in the centre depict *"Moses Drawing Water from the Rock"*, *"Moses and the Bronze Serpent"*, and the *"Miracle of the Manna"*. The smaller oval pieces illustrate episodes concerning Moses, Jonah, Elijah and Isaac. The walls show the *"Birth and Baptism of Christ"*, *"Miracles"*, the *"Temptations"*, the *"Last Supper"*, and the *"Resurrection"*.

Jacopo Tintoretto. Saint Roch in Glory   *Jacopo Tintoretto. Flight into Egypt*

Tintoretto's "Self-Portrait" is in the corner of the entrance wall. The Meeting Room was originally to have been decorated by Titian, but it was subsequently decided to hold a competition. Among the competitors were Veronese, Salviati, Zuccari and Tintoretto. To everyone's indignation Tintoretto won when he produced a finished painting, while the others offered cartoons only. Work was completed by 1566.

Jacopo Tintoretto. Christ going to Calvary

The centre of the coffered ceiling shows *"St Roch in Glory"* surrounded by other compartments with allegorical images that represent the major schools of Venice together with Cherubim and Virtues. A signed and dated *"Crucifixion"* (1565) hangs on the wall. The other canvases relate episodes in the *"Passion of Christ"*. The painting showing *"Christ Carrying the Cross"* and the *"Dead Christ"* are by Titian.

Basilica Santa Maria Gloriosa of the Frari

Saint Mary of the Friars (I Frari). Though building went on for a long time the church is remarkably homogeneous and represents, together with the Church of Saints John and Paul, one of the most complete and perfect examples of Venetian Gothic.

The original building, begun in 1250, was hardly finished, when the wealth of the Order of the Friars Minor of Saint Francis increased. They decided to build a new and larger edifice. Work commenced in 1340 from the apse end, and continued with the central nave toward the canal. The church was consecrated in 1469. It is built on

Basilica of Santa Maria Dei Frari. Cloisters

an Egyptian cross with three naves and seven chapels opening out from the apse end on the transept. The bell tower is erected at the point where the wall of the small first nave meets the transept, and is the work of Jacopo Celega and his sons Pietro and Paolo. It was finished by 1396. The ground plan of the first side of the church was enriched by the addition of the Corner Chapel in 1417, and the Emiliani Chapel in 1432. Through the main pointed-arched portal surmounted by a statue of the "Redeemer" by Alessandro Vittoria, one enters the church. The grandiosity of its interior is further accentuated by the towering columns of the nave supporting the high cross-vault. Between the last four columns as you go toward the transept, the friars' choir is placed in accordance with the liturgical tradition of the period. It is a wide and richly-decorated area with carved wooden choir stalls in three orders by Marco Cozzi (1468).

In the sacristy, added to the main building during the second half of the 15th century, is the priceless *"Virgin and Child with Cherubs, Musicians and Saints"* (1488) by Giovanni Bellini. The carved gilded frame was the work of Jacopo da Faenza and is in the form of the traditional triptych. As you re-enter the church from the sacristy, the Ca' Bernardo Chapel is on your right. It contains a polyptych by Bartolomeo Vivarini (1482) depicting the *"Madonna and Child with Saints"* and, higher up, "Christ on the Sarcophagus". The third chapel, of the Fiorentini, is thus called because the inhabitants of Florentine origin obtained permission in 1436 to erect this altar. (Could this have been a consequence of Cosimo de' Medici's period of exile in Padua from 1433-1434?)

The painted wooden sculpture of

Basilica of Santa Maria of the Frari. The Apse from the Campo San Rocco

Basilica of Santa Maria of the Frari.
Interior

Titian. Ca' Pesaro, altarpiece (det.)

"Saint John the Baptist" is a splendid work by Donatello.

The central chapel houses Titian's "Assumption" (1518). The Virgin rises to Heaven among a host of cherubs while the figure of the Eternal Father stands out on high. Next is the funeral monument to Jacopo Pesaro, who was Bishop of Cyprus when he commissioned Titian to paint the famous "Madonna of Ca' Pesaro" altarpiece. About 1669 B. Longhena framed the side door with a colossal monument to Doge Giovanni Pesaro, who had died ten years earlier. The composition is strictly Baroque, in the richness and abundance of its architectural and sculptural decoration.

Basilica of Santa Maria of the Frari, Main Altar. Titian, the Assumption

MURANO
BURANO
TORCELLO
LIDO
CHIOGGIA

Burano

Aereoporto Marco Polo

Murano Glass

MESTRE

MURA

Fusina

VENEZI

Chioggia

Albe

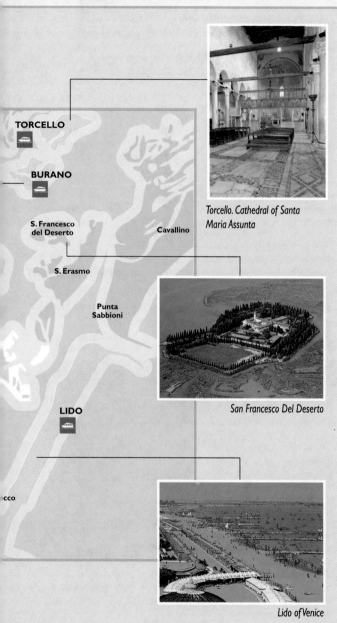

TORCELLO

BURANO

S. Francesco
del Deserto

Cavallino

S. Erasmo

Punta
Sabbioni

LIDO

cco

*Torcello. Cathedral of Santa
Maria Assunta*

San Francesco Del Deserto

Lido of Venice

At the Fondamenta Nuove waterbuses leave for Murano. On the way you will pass the City Cemetery on the two islands of San Michele and San Cristoforo della Pace now joined to form a single island.

At the cemetery boat-stop rises the **Church of San Michele** begun by Coducci about 1469. Built of white Istrian stone with light rustication, this is one of the earliest Renaissance buildings in Venice. Its three naves are revealed in the tripartite façade topped by

A View of the lagoon

semi-circular pediments, a theme used repeatedly by the artist, in subsequent religious and civic buildings such as the Church of San Zaccaria and Saint Mark's School in the Campo SS. Giovanni e Paolo. Next to this church is the Emiliani Chapel erected in 1530 by Guglielmo dei Grigi, from Bergamo, on a hexagonal plan.

Go ashore at Murano's last boat-stop and proceed along the Fondamenta which leads to the Glass Museum and the fine Church of St. Mary and Donatus.

A View of the lagoon with the Island of Torcello

Murano. Church and campanile of Santa Maria and Donato

Murano. Like other islands belonging to the entire complex of the lagoon, the island of Murano was inhabited by refugees from the mainland who had fled from the invading barbarians. At first it was dependent on the island city of Torcello, but by about the beginning of the 9th century it turned to Venice. It enjoyed a certain administrative autonomy, first of all under a Ducal Administrator and from 1272 under a Podestà. It had its own council and, just as in Venice, the founding families of this island were inscribed in their own Golden Book and enjoyed special privileges. A noble Venetian could marry the daughter of a master glass craftsman without losing his proper status. This island achieved its greatest splendour when Europe began to recognize the high quality and great value of Murano glass. No records indicate when glassmaking began at Murano, or anywhere in the Venetian Estuary. Handed down by the Romans, the art was probably brought here by travellers and spurred on by frequent contact with the Oriental world in the course of Venice's maritime trade. It is certain that skilful Saracen artists were working in glass in Syria from the 10th cent. on.

When the buildings of Venice were mainly made of wood the threat of

Aerial Views of the island of Murano

Murano. Glass Museum, Water Container

fire was so great that the Republic decreed that all glass factories should be transferred to Murano. Thus the island became the centre for all furnaces, and glass manufacture became its symbol and source of wealth.

The size of the population grew and the long-established palaces, churches and monasteries, with their rich and productive vineyards, flower gardens and kitchen gardens, now stood side by side with the new industry. The Giustiniani Palace or Palace of the Bishops of Torcello rises on the Fondamenta Marco Giustiniani. Originally a Gothic structure, it was rebuilt in 1689 and now houses the Glass Museum.

Glass Museum. On the ground floor is an exhibition of glass objects of archaeological origin; on the 1st floor, Murano glass dating from the 15th to the 19th century. An outstanding piece is the wedding cup made by the Baroviers (a famous family of glass manufacturers). Its smooth blue-violet surface is decorated with enamelled love scenes alternating with portraits of the bride and groom. In the centre of the main hall is a fine table centrepiece, a model of eighteenth-century landscape architecture.

By following the chronological arrangement of works in the exhibit, you will see the development of the glass-making art through the centuries.

Saint Mary and Donatus Church at the end of the fondamenta is of very ancient origin. Rebuilt in the 12th century, it was consecrated in 1140. The plan is basilican, with three naves, and the "ship's keel" ceiling dates back to the early 15th century. The magnificent polychrome mosaic floor and the large mosaic covering the bowl of the apse date from the construction of this church. Fantastically decorated with a false portico and deep niches in both the lower order and the upper loggia, the exterior part of the apse is in striking contrast with the simple basilican façade.

A View of Burano

The square bell tower stands apart in the campo and creates a splendid effect in this setting; an effect marred by the large modern Monument to the Fallen by the sculptor Martinuzzi.

Board the water bus for **Burano**. This island is heralded from a distance by its low, brightly-coloured buildings and tall, leaning campanile above the flat, pale surface of the lagoon. A visit to the island, though interesting from an architectural point of view, strikes us mainly for the glimpse of this fishing community's way of life. Here, the dialogue between man and the sea, begun centuries ago, still goes on. Its layout is, for the most part, still intact, and the low, humble, brightly-coloured buildings - like the original ones - wind along the canals and into the squares, with

Burano View

183

their familiar wells in an intimate exchange between the island and its lagoon setting.

Burano is also known for its lace, as renowned and world-famous as Murano's glass. On display in the small Museum is a collection of lace items.

Torcello. While approaching Torcello one is fascinated by its strange position, so isolated in the midst of the lagoon. Once an important political and commercial centre, it was founded by early refugees from the mainland. Remnants still exist of this, the lagoon's most ancient civilisation. The physical aspect has changed since then, as deposits of mud brought down by the rivers have

Torcello, Cathedral. A Tombstone

formed areas of marsh and bog. The area became malarial. Thus the archipelago rapidly declined, and the people left for other shores. All that remains as witness to the past splendour of this island are a few religious buildings: Santa Maria Assunta Church and Saint Fosca Church.

The Church of Santa Maria Assunta was first established in the 7th century, as the remains of a stone plaque dated 639 confirm. In 697 reconstruction and enlargement of the early church was undertaken, and it became the seat of a bishop. The lower part of the apse is the only section remaining of this edifice. In 864 it was again rebuilt: the structure became much larger both lengthwise - reaching as far as the ancient baptistery, of which only the foundation now remains - and in width, through the addition of two side aisles. The last radical restoration, during which the columns and capitals of the nave were renewed along with the wooden truss ceiling and the marble mosaic floor, dates back to 1000, when Orso, son of Doge Pietro II Orseolo, became Bishop of Torcello. The colonnade on the façade was renewed during the 14th and 15th centuries Note that the frames of the windows in the lateral walls are made of flat slabs of stone. Inside this church the bowl of the apse and the triumphal arch are covered with mosaics. At the top is the *"Virgin Mother of God"* and below is the *"Twelve Apostles"*. The *"Annunciation"* is depicted on

Torcello Island. The Devil's Bridge

Torcello. Cathedral of Santa Maria Assunta

the arch. Although their iconography belongs to the 7th century, these mosaics were probably made around the 12th century, though dating them with accuracy is difficult. On the right side of the apse the mosaics, inspired by those of Ravenna, represent *"Angels"* (set among arabesques of foliage), *"Christ Enthroned and Blessing"* and, on the lower level, *"Four Figures of Saints"*.

On the wall above the entrance is a grandiose mosaic: the *"Apotheosis of Christ and the Last Judgement"*.

In 864, Saint Fosca Church was built on a basilican plan and then rebuilt during the 10th century on a central plan. The portico extends along the five external sides of the octagon and was probably added later. The apse corresponds with the remaining three sides. Originally the architect intended to cover the building with a cupola, but a simple wooden covering was made instead. The base for the dome is all that remains of the project.

The Museum is in the small square in front of the church, and is the ancient town hall. It contains fragments of marble sculptures and bas-reliefs of Veneto-Byzantine art. In the Archives Palace are a number of sarcophagi, funeral steles

Cathedral of Santa Maria Assunta. Interior

San Francesco Del Deserto

and some Roman and Paleo-Christian inscriptions.

Next to Torcello lies the island of **San Francesco Del Deserto**. The evocative greenness of its tall cypresses gives you an idea of how similar places in the lagoon probably looked in past times. This island in inhabited by a community of the Conventual Order of Franciscan Friars Minor. The island gained renown when St. Francis was forced ashore here during a storm on his return from Syria. Enchanted by its simplicity, the Saint stayed on - as we may be tempted to do.

Beyond is the entrance to the port and the lagoon, once defended by two forts:

Lagoon Fishing

one on the Saint Nicholas side (known as Old Castle, now destroyed), and the other constructed in 1543, on the Saint Andrew side (called New Castle). Built to a design by the architect Michele Sanmicheli, the latter has now partly collapsed due to total lack of maintenance. Saint Nicholas forms the extreme northerly tip of the island of the Lido, a long, narrow strip of land closing off the lagoon as far as the Port of Alberoni. It then stretches past the villages of San Pietro in Volta and Pellestrina and onward, beyond the breakwater reaching the port of Chioggia.

In 1744 the Republic ordered construction of the murazzi, a vast defen-

San Francesco of the Deserto

sive sea-wall built of massive stone blocks. Conceived by the cosmographer Vincenzo Coronelli in 1716, it was built under the supervision of the Venetian mathematician Bernardino Zendrini and completed in 1782, shortly before the fall of the Republic. Though hard pressed for funds, it succeeded in finding the necessary resources for this colossal engineering project, which saved the city from the onslaughts of the sea.

The Church of San Nicolò, together with the Benedictine Monastery, was founded around 1043 on the aforementioned northern tip of the Lido. As Saint Mark's was under construction in 1071, Doge Domenico Selvo was elected here. The church was rebuilt in 1626, but its façade was not completed. Traces remain of the early church, of the alterations made in Gothic times and of the 1530 cloister.

A View of the Lagoon

The Lido. The island of the Lido was covered with rich vegetation and was not built up when the First World War broke out. Since then it has undergone rapid development, first in the central and northern sections and later in residential zones, which have extended as far as Malamocco on the southern tip. During the years between the two World Wars it became one of the best-known beaches in the world, and the favoured destination of a tourist élite attracted by the prestige associated with such manifestations as the Venice Film Festival. In addition, during those years the Municipal Gambling House (Casinò) was built on the Lido. During the winter months the Casino is transferred to the Vendramin-Calergi Palace on the Grand Canal in Venice proper.

Take a waterbus and stop at the Piazzale Santa Maria Elisabetta. A short walk down the Gran Viale takes you to the seashore. Numerous bathing establishments are located along the beach, which extends for a total distance of more than 7 km. Even the oldest hotels

San Lazzaro of the Armenians

Views of the Lido of Venice

situated along this shore were built during the period between the two World Wars. The Des Bains and Excelsior are well-known.

Towards the southern tip of the island rises the ancient centre of **Malamocco** (formerly Matamaucus), where in 742 the seat of government was transferred from Eraclea. Later, in 811, it was removed to Rivoalto or Rialto, giving origin to the history of Venice.

It seems that a tidal wave in 1107 entirely destroyed Matamaucus, soon rebuilt on its present site, a little farther removed from the sea. Maps and documents dating from 1150 call it Malamocco Novo. It enjoyed special privileges and had its own Podestà. The ancient Gothic style building of he Podestà stands in the square together with the church.

San Lazzaro of the Armenians. A community of Armenian monks inhabits the island today. Once it was set aside as a hospice for pilgrims who had fallen sick on their way to the Holy Land. Later it became a leprosarium dedicated to the patron saint of lepers, Saint Lazarus. In 1717 it was assigned to an Armenian nobleman, the monk Manug di Pietro (known as Mechitar) who had fled from Methoni when it was invaded by the Turks. He then founded a Benedictine monastery to shelter his fellow Armenian refugees, and this community became a famous centre of culture, linked by its origins to the Oriental world.

An excursion to **Chioggia**, whether by bus or by waterbus, provides the opportunity to take in the littoral, the Murazzi, should one stop off at S.Pietro in Volta, and the life of the fisherfolk. Chioggia today is a fishing port but tradition certainly dates back to Roman times. It was then called Fossa Clodia Major and Clodia Minor or Sottomarina.

The Chioggian War (1378-80) was a turning point in the history of the Republic. Besieged by the Genoese fleet, and on the point of yielding, Venice made a last effort and was rewarded with victory.

Among the ancient buildings in Chioggia, mention must be made of the church of S.Domenico, with Vittore Carpaccio's painting of St Paul (1520), the church of S.Giacomo and the Cathedral with its belltower. The Cathedral, with nave, two aisles and transept, is built on a Latin cross plan. Sottomarina is a modern seaside resort in constant evolution.

Chioggia

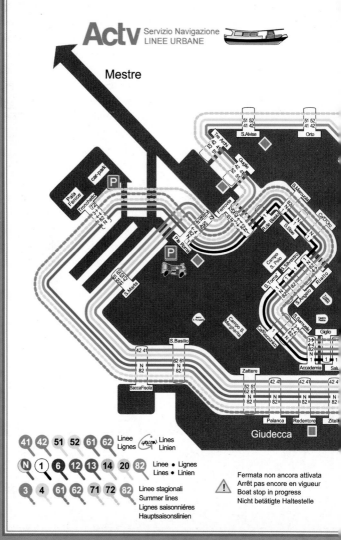

Actv

Servizio Navigazione
LINEE URBANE

Mestre

Legend:

41 42 51 52 61 62 — Linee / Lignes / Lines / Linien

N 1 6 12 13 14 20 82 — Linee • Lignes / Lines • Linien

3 4 61 62 71 72 82 — Linee stagionali / Summer lines / Lignes saisonniéres / Hauptsaisonslinien

⚠ Fermata non ancora attivata
Arrêt pas encore en vigueur
Boat stop in progress
Nicht betätigte Haltestelle

Actv

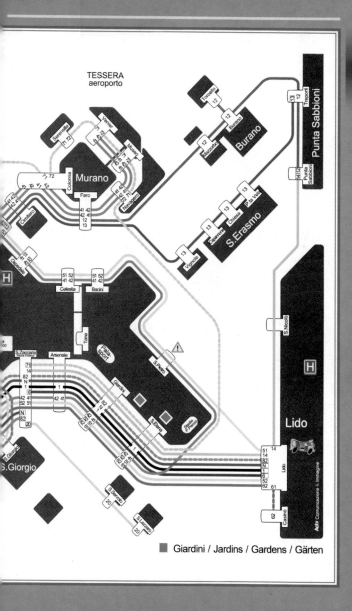

TESSERA
aeroporto

Serenella
Venier
Murano
Colonna
Murano
Faro
Cimitero
Navagero
Giudecca

Torcello
Mazzorbo
Burano

Punta Sabbioni
Treporti
Punta Sabbioni

S.Erasmo
Vignole
Capannone
Chiesa
P.ta Vela

Celestia
Bacini
Tana
Palla
sport
S.Pietro

S.Nicolò

H

Lido
Lido
Casinò

S.Zaccaria
Arsenale
Giardini
S.Elena
Stadio
P.Fenice

S.Giorgio
S.Servolo
S.Lazzaro

Giardini / Jardins / Gardens / Gärten

Actv Comunicazione & immagine

Venice

Graphic Design and Text:
Storti Edizioni Srl
Photography: Stortiarchiv,
Cameraphoto.

Printed: June 2001

STORTI EDIZIONI srl
Legal Address:
Via Tasso, 21 - Mestre-VENEZIA
Warehouse & Office: Via Brianza, 9/c
30030 - Oriago di Mira - VENEZIA

Tel. 041-5659057 / 58
Fax 041- 5631157
Internet: www.stortiedizioni.it
e-mail: edstort@tin.it

CONTENTS